# Everything Says, “Glory!”

# Everything Says, "Glory!"

## Science Exposes Darwinian Folklore

Jim Albright

# What Church Leaders Are Saying

The great strength of this book is the staggering number of relevant (and often shocking) quotations that Jim Albright has assembled from scientists and researchers representing an extraordinarily broad range of disciplines. That these statements come from both creationists and a great many evolutionists makes the book even more valuable. Believers will have their faith in the Creator God greatly strengthened. Skeptics will find their "faith" in evolution unexpectedly shaken. Whether you consider yourself well-informed on the creation/evolution debate or one who has read little on the subject, you'll find this book eye-opening.

**—*Donald S. Whitney***
*Professor of Biblical Spirituality and Associate Dean, The Southern Baptist Theological Seminary, Louisville, Kentucky; USA*

Jim Albright presents a straightforward and accessible critique of the myth of macro evolution. Pressing hard on the button of logical inference, supported by an array of notable authorities, he makes the case in a way that causes you to say, "How could it be possible to believe in evolution?" Father Darwin is still a daunting old man in the scientific community; Albright gives one more kick to his crutches. In his easy informal style, designed to simplify the complex, thinking persons will appreciate his candor and the absence of pretense. Creation leads to praise, as the Creator Himself claims. It does indeed! I'll share this helpful primer often.

**—*Jim Elliff***
*President of Christian Communicators Worldwide and a founding pastor of Christ Fellowship of Kansas City, Missouri, USA*

The debate between Darwinian evolution and biblical Christianity continues, but certainly not in a fair-minded way. But alas, there are those in the unbelieving world of scientific endeavor who have . . . acknowledged that Darwin and his ilk have . . . fatal principles within their own "belief" systems. Pastor Jim Albright, in this short book on the subject, quotes voluminously from both those who admit such weaknesses, and . . . those who believe a Creator God is gloriously behind earthly life's first beginning. . . . Therefore, my advice to you, dear reader, is this: Whether you are currently on the one side or the other of this important origins debate—or perhaps even somewhere in between—sincerely contemplate what you find in these pages.

***—Lance Quinn***

*Senior Pastor Bethany Church on the Hill, Thousand Oaks, California, USA*

Jim Albright has provided a great service to those who might wonder about the "science" of evolution. His book covers many topics and questions that people are asking today. Each chapter utilizes scientific and logical evidence to expose the lie that evolution is. Albright has sifted through the writings of many scholars and put their findings in a book that is understandable by everyone, regardless of their scientific understanding. In a sense, he has put the cookies on the table where everyone can reach them. Best of all, Albright's book points us all back to the wonder of the Creator whose glory is revealed in every aspect of His creation!

***—Jim Ehrhard***

*Ph.D. of Theology, Professor at Kiev Theological Seminary, Kiev, Ukraine*

A deep book written in a wonderful, almost conversational level, almost as if you are discussing it around the kitchen table at the end of the day. And yet, if you will allow it, this book draws you in and convinces you—not that you were right but that God is who He is, wonderful and glorious, and as you finish it you worship God all the more and your tongue and heart are loosed to speak what you know is true with confidence and assurance.

***—Alan Johnston***

*Minister in the Presbyterian Church of Ireland over twenty years*

"Everything says, 'Glory!'" is a great resource for the church. Tackling the creation vs evolution debate, this book strikes a great balance between technical detail and a layman-type synopsis. It will bolster the believer's confidence in the biblical account of creation and provide information to assist in defending it in the realm of natural science. This book, like the reversal on Haman as recorded in the biblical book of Esther, takes atheism's attempt to exterminate God and turns it around to exterminate atheism.

***—Brad Vaden***
*Pastor of Grace Baptist Church, Scott, Arkansas, USA*

Jim Albright's new book *Everything says, "Glory!"* says what you've waited your whole life for someone to say but lacked the spine to say: we live in GOD's world—period. Not only do we live in God's world but every consideration that man can make regarding God's world proves it—regardless of what so-called modern-day science says. The best part of the book isn't that it demolishes the modern-day myth of a world spawned from nothing by nothing for nothing. The best part of this book is that it will provoke you to a whole new level of worship of the Creator for whom and by whom Creation is. This book will remove all obstacles from your view, and it will clear up any confusion that has come into your mind so that a view of the One True God of His world can emerge unhindered. Come, reader. Worship and serve the wonderful Creator God that Jim re-presents to you.

***—Keith Jones***
*Founding Pastor of Centro Veritas Church, Milan, Italy*

When, in the future, I need an example of what it looks like to love God with all of my mind, Jim Albright will stand ready in my thoughts as "Exhibit A." Obviously, Pastor Albright's work goes well beyond demonstrating how deeply his mind is affected with love for God; yet, it displays the fruit of applying one's mind to the pursuit of God-focused worship. Indeed, as the title declares, *Everything Says, "Glory!"*, the author's "grey matter" not only says GLORY; it compels the reader to do the same. I appreciate this book's synthesis of thoughtful, honest, subject-matter experts as they describe uncomfortable truths (for Darwinian theorists) regarding the important topics of cosmology and human origin. Read this book closely; think deeply; observe inquisitively; worship passionately!

—***Doug Richey***

*Senior Pastor of Pisgah Baptist Church, Excelsior Springs, Missouri, USA*

This beautifully efficient book gives a great deal of help and hope to believers trying to paddle their way down the river of our post-truth culture. With a treasure of quotable science, Albright steers us toward the calming and invigorating realities surrounding the one, true "Genius-Creator." A true go-to reference book for quotes and insights for any believer.

—***Dow Welsh***

*Pastor of Holland Avenue Baptist Church, Cayce, South Carolina, USA*

If I had ten dollars to spend on a good book on God and Darwinism, I would spend it on this great book that my friend Jim has written for Christians who want to know more about the glory of God in everything He did. When you finish the book, your heart will start to praise Him for His power.

—***Andrea Artioli***

*Founding Pastor of Sola Grazia Church, Montova, Italy*

First Edition: 2018

ISBN: 978-0-9965168-8-4

[LSI-20190125-TS16a]

Great Writing Publications
www.greatwriting.org
Taylors, SC, USA

# Contents

# Acknowledgments

I praise my Creator-God for the intoxicating miracle of life and the inexhaustible wonder of being. "Who is like You among the gods, O LORD? Who is like You, majestic in holiness, awesome in praises, working wonders?"[1]

I do want to salute the brave scientists who come to their work every day with genuine integrity—the men and women who simply follow the evidence wherever it leads, no matter the ideological implications. Sadly, Charles Darwin has been canonized by much of the scientific establishment; consequently, dissent can be costly. So, my hat is off to these plucky professionals who tell us the truth, no matter how unfashionable or uncomfortable it might be.

I also wish to thank my best friend and wife, Karen. She not only wields a first-rate editor's pen; she patiently listens to me incessantly talk about whatever topic I'm currently researching and writing about. Trust me, she could tell you a thing or two about Darwinian folklore!

And many thanks to the stellar group of pastors, seminary professors, and missionaries who have endorsed the book. These men have acknowledged both the worship-provoking aspect of this work as well as its edifying merit.

Lastly, but not least by any means, my thanks to Jim Holmes of Great Writing for his editing and design work. He has smoothed out all the rough places to create a better read for you.

[1] Exodus 15:11.

# About the Cover

So, why the peacock feather on the cover? Because Charles Darwin hated it. He wrote, "The sight of a feather in a peacock's tail, whenever I gaze at it, makes me sick!"[1]

The obvious problem was that he did not know how to plausibly explain this large, mathematically patterned, jewel-colored, gratuitous display of beauty in evolutionary terms. A peacock tail can stand five feet high. And all those cumbersome feathers are most inconvenient regarding the chief survival-of-the-fittest issue—namely, not being eaten. This was no small dilemma for Mr. Darwin.

In keeping with his general approach to science, Darwin concocted a story. Give the man credit. He knew how to weave a narrative. This is, of course, the foremost skill of his disciples. Storytelling is far less bothersome than engaging in the exacting rigors of real science.

Darwin proposed a theory of sexual selection. That is, peahens prefer peacocks with the best tails. Best meaning, the biggest and most colorful. The gaudier the tail, Darwin surmised, the better the peacock would fare with the peahens, and consequently pass on more of the flamboyant plumage genes to male offspring.

Oops. Yeah, this doesn't actually happen. This is where storytelling, as opposed to truly doing science, puts one in a bit of a bind. A "seven-year study that observed 268 matings"[2] conducted by scientists *seeking to confirm* Darwin's theory, found that peacock sexual selection based upon the coolest tail, is, and sorry, I couldn't resist borrowing Ph.D. David Catchpoole's quote, "poppycock."[3]

The "tail tale"[4] is the perfect parable of Darwinian evolutionary theory. It's all just unsubstantiated anecdotes. Regarding the macro-Darwinian hypothesis, there is no hard data. Zero. But oh, what a fanciful myth of unparalleled imagination has been fabricated for the incurious and unwary!

Darwin hated the peacock feather. It makes no evolutionary sense. Exactly!

[1] Charles Darwin and Francis Darwin, The Life and Letters of Charles Darwin, including an Autobiographical Chapter, Vol. 2 (New York: D. Appleton, 1911), 90-91.

[2] Catchpoole, D., Peacock tail tale failure, creation.com/tale, 2008. (Creation 31(2):56–Jun 2008).

[3] Catchpoole, D., https://creation.com/peacock-poppycock (Creation 29(2):56 - Mar 2007).

[4] Ibid.

# The Earth Is Yours

Your voice it thunders, The oaks start twisting
The forest sounds with cedars breaking
The waters see You and start their writhing
From the depths a song is rising
Now it's rising from the ground
Holy, holy, holy, holy Lord
The earth is Yours and singing
Holy, holy, holy, holy Lord
The earth is Yours
The earth is Yours

Your voice it thunders, The ground is shaking
The mighty mountains, now are trembling
Creation sees You, and starts composing
The fields and trees, they start rejoicing
And now it's rising from the ground
Now it's rising from the ground
Hear us crying out
Hear us crying out
Holy, holy, holy, holy Lord
The earth is Yours and singing
Holy, holy, holy, holy Lord
The earth is Yours and singing
Holy, holy, holy, holy Lord
The earth is Yours
The earth is Yours
The earth is Yours

# Prologue

Cutting-edge science has revealed that Darwinian evolutionary theory is dead.

This is beyond doubt for any knowledgeable person. Thankfully, the whole silly, nonsensical affair is over. The hypothesis can simply no longer survive the unrelenting assault of facts and logic. Darwinists have truly become the quintessential science-deniers. They are, indeed, the flat-earthers of the twenty-first century! I know you haven't seen this on *60 Minutes,* or read it in *The New York Times,* but I don't suppose very many of us are in any real danger of encountering discriminating journalism.

Of course, the Darwinian fundamentalists will continue to pontificate and rail for they have never been much bothered with evidence and intelligible inference. Regarding state-of-the-art science, these two borrowed quotes bring us up to speed quite nicely . . .

> "The fall of Darwinism will be the big story of the early 21st century—learn about it now and be ahead of the curve!"[1]
> *Phillip E. Johnson, Author and Professor, University of California, Berkley*

> ". . . no informed person will ever again honestly say that Darwin's theory flows straight from the data."[2]
> *Michael Behe, Ph.D. Biology, Professor of Biochemistry, Lehigh University*

The informed, intellectually honest scientist knows that these statements are true. Sadly, many do not seem to possess the mettle to speak against this uncritically favored, fanatically held, and entrenched hypothesis. The guardians of evolutionary orthodoxy don't always play nice. Therefore, many scientists who question Darwinian groupthink simply keep their heads down. It can literally be a career-ending objection.

But . . . there are a few valiant men and women who have put down the Kool-Aid and are diligently following the evidence where it leads. Please note, this book is not about what I think. This book is about what these first-class scientists and thinkers see in, and infer from, the data. Yes, science is revealing that the God hypothesis is indispensable.

The quote widely attributed to George Orwell flawlessly fits our day relative to the pseudo-scientific creation myths known as Big Bang and Darwinian evolution. "During times of universal deceit, telling the truth becomes a revolutionary act."

Christian, as a lover and follower of Jesus Christ in a fallen world, you are the consummate revolutionary. Your family needs to hear what objective scientists are discovering. Your fellow church members need to hear it. Your colleagues and neighbors need to hear it. Read. Be informed. And after you have worshiped, push back the darkness with the soul-gripping truth of a breath-taking Creator-God! This is, indeed, every Christian's high privilege and happy labor for the few moments we have left on the planet—to proclaim His truth by echoing the words of that renown Jewish poet, "Everything says, 'Glory!'"[3]

* * *

"We are destroying speculations and every lofty thing raised up against the knowledge of God. . . ."[4]
*Paul, God's Apostle*

[1] Cited in David Berlinski, *The Deniable Darwin* (Seattle, WA: Discovery Institute Press, 2009), 101.

[2] Michael Behe Foreword, Phillip Johnson, *Darwin on Trial* (Downers Grove, IL: InterVarsity Press, 2010), 13.

[3] Psalm 29:9.

[4] 2 Corinthians 10:5.

“The truth is like a lion.
You don’t need to defend it.
Let it loose.
It will defend itself.”

*Augustine*

Fifth-Century Christian Theologian

# Unpacking the Title

## Everything Says, "Glory!"

### Science Exposes Darwinian Folklore

**Everything** *pron.* **1.** All things or factors that exist . . .

**Says** *v.* **1.** To utter aloud; pronounce. **3.** To state; declare.

**Glory** *n.* **1.** Great honor, praise . . . renown. **4.** Adoration, praise and thanksgiving offered in worship. **5.** Majestic beauty and splendor; resplendence. **7.** The height of achievement . . .

**Science** *n.* **1.** The observation, identification, description, experimental investigation, and theoretical explanation of natural phenomena. **4.** Knowledge . . . gained through experience.

**Expose(s)** *v.* **1. b.** To lay open **2.** To subject to the action of light. **4. a.** To make known. **b.** To reveal . . .

**Darwinian** *adj.* A theory of biological evolution developed by Charles Darwin and others, stating that species of plants and animals develop through natural selection of variations that increase the organism's ability to survive and reproduce.

**Folklore** *n.* **1** . . . legends and tales of a people . . . **3.** a body of widely accepted but specious notions . . .

* * *

*All things or factors that exist . . . utter, pronounce, state, and declare. . .* the *great honor, renown, adoration, and praise offered in worship to* the Creator in the . . . *majestic beauty, splendor, resplendence* and *height of achievement* in His creative work. *The observation, identification, description, experimental investigation, and theoretical explanation of natural phenomena . . . lays open to the action of light, to make known,* and *to reveal. . .* that the *theory of biological evolution developed by Charles Darwin . . .* is the stuff of *legends and tales, a body of widely accepted but specious notions.*[1]

[1] All definitions are from *The American Heritage Dictionary* (Boston: Houghton Mifflin Co., 1985).

# Introduction

". . . Holy, Holy, Holy, is the LORD of hosts,
The whole earth is full of His glory."

*Isaiah 6:3*

David is watching a thunderstorm pass through Lebanon, and worship is rising in his heart and mind. It's the thinking person's instinctive response to the genius, power, complexity, symmetry, beauty, design, and scale revealed in the created order. David's praise is recorded in Psalm 29:

> Ascribe to the LORD glory and strength. Ascribe to the LORD the glory due to His name. . . . The God of glory thunders. . . . The voice of the LORD is powerful. The voice of the LORD is majestic. The voice of the LORD breaks the cedars. . . . The voice of the LORD hews out flames of fire. The voice of the LORD shakes the wilderness. . . . Everything says, "Glory!"[1]

David sees it. He feels it. He knows it. It's unmistakable. There's glory. There's wonder. There's awe. There is a deep, visceral awareness of the Transcendent. His soul is shouting, *"God!"* Not just any god, but a Creator-God of unsearchable greatness,[2] before whom the earth trembles and the mountains melt like wax.[3]

David recognizes what C.S. Lewis calls the "divine, magical, terrifying, and ecstatic reality in which we all live."[4] The created order demands the God hypothesis. He cannot not be there. Lest this overwhelming intuition of glory be willfully and proactively "suppressed,"[5] worship is the only reasonable response afforded to humanity. The intellectually honest person must and will stand in utter amazement!

It's David's response. He is filled with wonderment, as well he should be, at the Author of such a magnificent display of power. But, in one sense, it's only *just* a thunderstorm. You and I have so much more insight into the ubiquitous and inestimable power resident within the known universe.

## The Hiding of His Power

You and I have seen the pictures from the Hubble Space Telescope. We have peered 13+ billion light years into the "deep space field."[6] We know that one present estimate of galaxies—not stars, or planets, but galaxies—in the known cosmos is 2 trillion![7] We also know that our sun is a gigantic fusion reactor with a core temperature of 27 million degrees Fahrenheit and that about one million earths could fit inside of it. We know, too, that UY Scuti, the largest known star, has a volume 5 billion times that of our sun! The mind boggles at the sheer, unquantifiable enormity of energy pulsating throughout the natural realm. And this seemingly endless, even redundant, display of might is, as God's prophet writes, the "hiding of His power."[8] Yeah, David got it right: "Glory!"

## The Creator's Intellectual Property

David was not only astonished at what he saw. He was amazed at what he was. He understood he was "fearfully and wonderfully made."[9] I've always loved how David finished that thought. He wrote, "wonderful are Your works, and my soul knows it very well."[10] The knowing changes everything, doesn't it? We have no doubt. We have no "excuse."[11] We know, "It is He who has made us and not we ourselves."[12] Consequently, we comprehend that we are not cosmic free agents. We are, in the very least, whether we know and love Him or not, an awesome Creator's intellectual property.

David is marveling, as well he should, at the Designer of such a being as he. But by twenty-first century standards, David knows next to nothing of the unfathomable miracle that is the human body. It is estimated to take about "60 zettabytes (60 with 21 zeros after) of information"[13] to build a human being. Within the DNA in each one of the estimated 40-100 trillion cells in your body (except red blood cells), are 3.5 billion characters of information; the instructions for building you. Yes, that's a lot! So where did all that code come from? A good guess would be, not from nothing, and not by chance.

David, who didn't know a fraction of what you and I know, knew this. He was a great deal more than mere chemistry and biology. And no matter how adamantly modern academia and the media tell us we are little more than grown-up germs, we intuitively know it's a lie. We know there is something more, something bigger, something meaningful, something beautiful, something magnificent . . . Someone glorious! We know there is something more awe-inspiring than the net effect of a long chain of chemical reactions, random variation, and natural selection. Biological and cognitive realities, rational deliberation, logical deduction, and commonsense will not allow the thinking person to embrace materialistic reductionism.

## Bumping into Wonder

Naturalism and materialism (the philosophy that nothing exists except matter and its movements and modifications) simply can't explain what each of us feels as we drink in the wonder we bump into every single day of our lives. We wake up to a conscious mind brimming with feelings, hopes, dreams, and creative instincts. If we're paying any attention at all, we intuit the Divine at every turn and, indeed, feel the impulse to bow down. We kiss our soul mate and taste the passionate rush of deep romance, love, and intimacy. We hear Beethoven's Ninth Symphony and know our souls were designed to soar with joy. We watch a perfect moonrise and a breathtaking sunset, and we know we're made to not only recognize, but savor majestic beauty. We look into the Milky Way on a clear night and we sense that infinity awaits. Yes, David is right every single day in every single circumstance: "Everything says, 'Glory!'"

Satan hates this. It's why he and his minions have expended so much pseudo-intellectual capital in seeking to discredit the

Genesis creation account. If the words "In the beginning God created the heavens and the earth"[14] are true, we have a Creator before whom we are accountable with all the obvious implications extending into a timeless eternity. If Genesis 1:1 is not true, not much else really matters. Mankind is an inexplicable, meaningless, pathetic, doomed, cosmic accident; all dressed up with nowhere to go. Satan knows what's at stake in the first two chapters of Genesis. Ultimately, everything is a divinely wrought miracle, or nothing is. The adversary desperately wants you to buy into the latter. He wants to steal the glory you and I were created to see, taste, savor, enjoy, and inherit!

## The Radically God-Centered Point of Creation

Christian, our testimony is that the created order is the miraculous handiwork of a breathtakingly awesome God. The apostle Paul writes, "For by Him [Jesus Christ] all things were created, both in the heavens and on earth, visible and invisible . . . all things have been created through Him and for Him.[15] Understand, everything is not only *from* Him; everything is *for* Him, and, of course, everything is *about* Him! Yes, that is the radically God-centered, bottom-line message of Creation and the gospel. Jesus Christ is the point! He's always been the point! He will always be the point!

It's why the Genesis creation account matters. It's why it matters a lot. It's why it's non-negotiable for the "born-again"[16] Bible believer. This is all about Jesus Christ. That's why the Genesis account is relentlessly attacked in the world. Because it's all about the glory of the Son of Man. And, as every born-again soul knows and understands, the world "hates"[17] the biblical Jesus. The world is always working if not to mythologize the God-Man, then, in the very least, to marginalize Him. The world doesn't mind so much if it can relegate Him to the status of religious icon. But He is never, under any circumstance, to be acknowledged as the supernatural, personal, eternal, omnipotent, omniscient, galaxy-breathing, life-giving, cosmos-upholding-and-sustaining Creator-God!

## Nonsense Is Nonsense

The adherents of scientism (the view that science is the only way to truth) tell us that God is an unnecessary and unwarranted presupposition. They tell us that stuff just happens. You know, sometimes there's nothing, and then, unaccountably, there's everything! Yeah, I know. But it's actually what this secular religion asserts. Arguably the most famous scientist of the modern era, Stephen Hawking, wrote...

> because there is a law such as gravity, the universe will create itself from nothing. . . . Spontaneous creation is the reason there is something rather than nothing, why the universe exists, why we exist. It is not necessary to invoke God to . . . set the universe going.[18]

I know; a self-creating universe. And not just your run-of-the-mill universe, mind you—but a seemingly infinite space-time-matter-energy-information-intelligence universe replete with mystifying intricacy, regularity, equilibrium, order, elegance, beauty, and precision fine-tuning. You're right: it's a perfect rabbit out of a hat. Oh, without the rabbit. And oh, without the hat. And yes, of course, without a Magician. Oxford math professor John Lennox sums up this attempt to yank a universe out of nothing better than anyone: ". . .nonsense remains nonsense, even when talked by world-famous scientists."[19]

## Darwin's Pseudo-Science

This brings me to Charles Darwin, the nineteenth-century English naturalist who is known as the father of the "particles to people"[20] evolutionary hypothesis. It is not my assertion that Charles Darwin and others were, or are, consciously waging war on Jesus Christ. It may be true. It may well not be true. But that is ultimately beside the point. This book is not about Darwin's theology; it's about his science. And his science has proven to be little more than anecdotal observation, exaggerated inference, unsophisticated speculation, and just some good old-fashioned storytelling.

Obviously, Darwin was keenly aware of the substantial empirical problems his theory was running into early on. As science has progressed into the twenty-first century, those difficulties have only multiplied . . . exponentially. They are, in fact, insurmountable. In my reading, I have seen more than one scientist question whether Darwin, given the current avalanche of evidence against his thesis, would continue to hold to it.

Macro-Darwinian evolution is dead. It doesn't work. It was pseudo-science in the nineteenth century and it has only gotten uglier. It's not science at all. It's a philosophical worldview through which data is interpreted. It is certainly more akin to religion than to science. There are no facts proving macroevolution. Zero. Nada. They do not exist. Not one single, solitary, indisputable fact corroborates the fantastic efficacy attributed to biological evolution. So, you may ask, why do people believe it? The simple answer is this: because they want to. They want to believe it. So, they see it. It's the classic example of a conclusion in search of evidence.

## Science Done Right Points to God

I know the world gets mad at Bible-believing Christians about this. I know they get red-faced about it. I know they think we're knuckle-dragging fundamentalists. I know they call us ignorant rubes and science-deniers. But the truth of the matter is this: we have the science! We have the data! Darwinists concoct fanciful stories out of thin air, while creationists deal with hard facts. Cambridge Ph.D. Stephen C. Meyer said it perfectly: "Science done right points to God."[21]

Unfortunately, this is news to some readers—that we, as Christians, not only hold the only credible theological explanation for a glory-infused cosmos, but that we, indeed, hold the only plausible scientific explanation. It's my sense that many readers don't know that is true. It's why I've labored outside my field in preparing this book. I'm an evangelical, Bible-believing preacher but I did not write this book to make the theological argument for a Creator. I wrote this book to enlighten you about brilliant scientists who are making the empirical argument for Him. These men and women get it. They see Him in the data. It screams at them from their microscopes and their telescopes: "Everything says, 'Glory!'"

## Why Read This Book?

So why read a book mostly about evolution written by a really, really smalltime preacher? I would humbly suggest two reasons.

*One,* science is not some mystical, ethereal realm that only the lab-coated priesthood of scientism can understand. I know they like to project and preserve that illusion, but it's not true. Everyone, to one degree or another, is a scientist. We observe and we learn. Science can be accurately defined simply as "Knowledge . . . gained through experience."[22] That's really all there is to it. It's what Cambridge Ph.D. Douglas Axe calls "common science." Axe writes, ". . . mastery of technical subjects isn't at all needed in order for us to know the answer to the big question."[23] He's right.

*Secondly,* I am only relaying information I've gleaned from broad reading on the topic. There are many excellent books that expose macroevolutionary science for what it is—a feeble, fanciful, and uninteresting creation myth. But most of those volumes are 200+ pages that sometimes get into the technical weeds. Most Christians simply will not take the time to read these works. I pray my service to the reader is to simply and succinctly pass on what eminent scientists are now saying and which clearly debunks the Darwinian folklore that pollutes our culture.

## The Payoff in Reading This Book

As already stated, this book is not about what I think; it's about what scientists know—brilliant, erudite, competent, degreed men and women who are diligently and painstakingly seeking truth and, consequently, discovering and documenting the heartfelt sentiments of David in Psalm 29. I will quote these men and women liberally throughout the book. It's the payoff for you in reading this work. What are real scientists and thinkers saying about the materialistic, Darwinian paradigm? Here is a small sampling. . .

❖ "Evolutionism is a fairy-tale for grown-ups. This theory has helped nothing in the progress of science. It is useless."[24]
*Professor Louis Bounoure, Ph.D.*
*Director of Research, French National Center of Scientific Research*

❖ "If Darwin's theory of evolution has little to contribute to the content of the sciences, it has much to offer their ideology. It is the creation myth of our time. . . ."[25]
*David Berlinski, Ph.D.*
*Senior Fellow at the Discovery Institute*

❖ "In Darwinian theory . . . miracles become the rule: events with an infinitesimal probability could not fail to occur. . . . There is no law against daydreaming, but science must not indulge in it."[26]
*Pierre Grasse, Ph.D.*
*Chair of Evolution at the Sorbonne*

❖ "Nine-tenths of the talk of evolutionists is sheer nonsense, not founded on observation and wholly unsupported by facts. This museum is full of proofs of the utter falsity of their views. . . . It is easy enough to make up stories of how one form gave rise to another. . . . But such stories are not part of science, for there is no way of putting them to the test."[27]
*Colin Patterson, Ph.D.*
*Senior Paleontologist, British Museum of Natural History*

- ❖ "[Neo-Darwinism is] a minor twentieth-century religious sect within the sprawling religious persuasion of Anglo-Saxon biology."[28]
  *Lynn Margulis, Ph.D.*
  *Professor of Biology at the University of Massachusetts*

- ❖ "The evidence for Darwinism is not only grossly inadequate, it is systematically distorted. I'm convinced that sometime in the not-too-distant future. . .people will look back in amazement and say, 'How could anyone have believed this?' Darwinism is merely materialistic philosophy masquerading as science. . . ."[29]
  *Jonathan Wells, Ph.D.*
  *Molecular and Cell Biology*

## Learn, Worship, Believe, Tell!

Christian, I want to inform you if I can, but mostly, I want to inspire you!

*First,* I want you to worship. I mean—really worship. If you read this book and think deeply about your very present Genius-Creator and His astonishing handiwork, you will. And somewhere in these pages, several readers will even begin to believe *more*. Well, that's what happened to me as I researched and wrote the book. Perhaps some readers will discover that they simply must join me in savoring the presence of our empirically "here" God. Yeah, I know, you're a "seriously-joyful and joyfully-serious,"[30] Word-doing Christian who doesn't need to believe *more*. But friend, this is not about need; this is about awe! Awe is good! Awe is very good! Awe is essential. It is necessary. It is our delight, our worship, and our fuel. It is mandatory for every lover of Jesus Christ! Awe is our license to live our faith "with glad reckless joy"[31] no matter what today brings!

*Secondly,* I want you to stop holding your tongue in the public square. I want you to begin to humbly and joyfully share the ecstatic joy of the unavoidable implications of a spectacular Creator-God. As stated in the prologue, everyone you know needs to hear this! The entire world needs to hear this! You must speak. You must help those in your orbit reject the nihilism that logically and inevitably results from the materialistic, Darwinian worldview. We must not let the "god of this world"[32] go unchallenged in his quest to blind our families and friends to the obvious, irrefutable, and clearly observable truth of David's happy exclamation in Psalm 29:9, "Everything says, 'Glory!'"

* * *

"Nothing that is, just is. Everything exists for a grand, vertical purpose . . . God created the physical world to be mnemonic, to help us daily remember that we are not alone, that we are not at the center . . . . Physical things are meant to remind us of the grandeur and glory of the One who created all things, set them in motion, and keeps them together by the awesome power of His will.[33]

*Paul David Tripp, Christian Pastor, Counselor, and Author*

# Notes: Introduction

[1] Psalm 29: 1-9, (Excerpts).
[2] Psalm 145:3.
[3] Psalm 97:4-5.
[4] C. S. Lewis, as quoted by Colin Duriez, The *A-Z of C. S. Lewis* (Oxford, England, Lion Books, 2013), 216.
[5] Romans 1:18.
[6] William R. Newcott, "Hubble's Eye on the Universe," *National Geographic*, April,1997, 10-11.
[7] Marina Koren, "The Universe Just Got 10 Times More Interesting," *The Atlantic*, October 14, 2016, accessed May 15, 2018, https://www.theatlantic.com/science/archive/2016/10/so-many-galaxies/504185/.
[8] Habakkuk 3:4.
[9] Psalm 139:14.
[10] Ibid.
[11] Romans 1:19-20.
[12] Psalm 100:3.
[13] Casey Chan, "How Many Gigabytes Does It Take to Build a Human?" Sploid, July 4, 2014, accessed April 20, 2018, https://sploid.gizmodo.com/how-many-gigabytes-does-it-take-to-make-a-human-1600123081.
[14] Genesis 1:1.
[15] Colossians 1:16.
[16] John 3:3.
[17] John 15:18.
[18] Cited in John Lennox, *God and Stephen Hawking* (Oxford, England: Lion Hudson, 2014), 16.
[19] Ibid., 32.
[20] Jonathan Sarfati, *The Greatest Hoax on Earth* (Atlanta, GA: Creation Book Publishers, 2010), 9.
[21] Cited in Lee Strobel, *The Case for a Creator* (Grand Rapids, MI: Zondervan, 2004), 77.
[22] "Science," *The American Heritage Dictionary* (Boston: Houghton Mifflin Co., 1985).
[23] Douglas Axe, *Undeniable* (New York: Harper One, 2016), 10.
[24] Cited in *The Advocate*, March 8, 1984, 17.
[25] David Berlinski, The *Devil's Delusion* (New York, NY: Basic Books, 2008), 190.
[26] Pierre-Paul Grasse, *Evolution of Living Organisms: Evidence for a New Theory of Transformation* (New York: Academic Press, 1978), 103.
[27] Cited in John Blanchard, *Does God Believe in Atheists?* (Darlington, UK: Evangelical Press, 2000), 114.

[28] Cited in C. Mann, *'Lynn Margulis; Science's Unruly Mother'*, in *Science*, No. 252, pp. 378-81.
[29] Cited in Strobel, 65.
[30] John Piper, Pastor, Sermon at Bethlehem Baptist Church, Minneapolis, Minnesota.
[31] Oswald Chambers, *My Utmost For His Highest Daily Devotional Journal* (Uhrichsville, OH: Barbour Books, 1992), March 28th entry.
[32] 2 Corinthians 4:4.
[33] Paul David Tripp, *Awe* (Wheaton, Il: Inter-Varsity, 2015), 66-68.

# ~one~

## The
## Science of a Fiction

"I grew up believing in this myth [evolution] and I have felt—I still feel—its almost perfect grandeur. Let no one say we are an unimaginative age: neither the Greeks nor the Norsemen ever invented a better story."[1]

*C. S. Lewis, Oxford Fellow, Cambridge Professor, Christian Apologist*

"The more one studies paleontology, the more certain one becomes that evolution is based on faith alone; exactly the same sort of faith which is necessary to have when one encounters the great mysteries of religion."[2]

*L. T. More, Ph.D. Paleontologist, University of Chicago*

"I would rather believe in fairies than in such wild speculation."[3]

*Ernst Chain, Biochemist, Fellow of the Royal Society, Nobel Prize Winner*

". . . Science boasts intellectual openness as its core virtue. . . . But when openness gives way to dogma on any particular scientific claim, we're left with something more like bad religion than good science."[4]

*Douglas Axe, Ph.D., Molecular Biologist*

Well, at the outset, let me confess that in discovering I had been duped in both high school and college bothers me a whole lot more than just a little. I mean, I always showed up for class with good intent—well, almost always. I just wanted someone to teach me some science. To simply be honest and clear. You know, I expected to be educated and informed in my science classes, not indoctrinated. I expected evidence, not speculation. I expected integrity, not duplicity. I expected facts, not tenets of faith dressed up in the guise of knowledge. Really, who knew ideology had been smuggled into biology? How would a naïve, gullible, and, yes, habitually distracted teenager even know?

Imagine my disillusionment in discovering that I had assumed way too much in school. I quite naturally believed that my teachers were goodwilled, well informed, and trustworthy professionals who knew what they were talking about and would teach me fact-based science. It was several decades later that I discovered there was a lot more going on in those classes than met the eye. In fact, those classes had doubled as a course in naturalism as it relates to the "microbes to man" Darwinian hypothesis. I was instructed that evolution is in the data. I had to find out for myself that it's only in the dogma.

## They Did Not Know Half What They Claimed to Know

Regarding his adolescent science instruction, journalist Peter Hitchens had the same experience I had. He writes, ". . . I was simply given the impression by adults that these things were the case, and that this was all settled forever." He continues, "They did not know half the things they claimed to know."[5] Yeah, that! Unfortunately, things have not changed much since my high school days as Ph.D. Jonathan Wells warns: "Students and the public are being systematically misinformed about the evidence for evolution."[6] Ph.D. John Baumgardner is a bit more pointed in saying that there has been "glaring scientific fraud for the past century"[7] in both biology and geology.

In truth, I struggled mightily with the title of this initial chapter. I think *Science of a Fiction* nails it, but I could have easily gone with *Data or Dogma, Proof or Preference, Fact or Folklore.* The word folklore is a perfect fit. It's the precise word for the macroevolutionary paradigm. It's why I found a way to get it into the subtitle. Folklore is generally made up of legends and tales of a people group that are often widely believed but are more akin to fairy tales. It's just like science class at university!

And sorry, I feel like I've already cheated you in that I had to choose four introductory quotes from a seemingly limitless supply—comments from renowned scholars and scientists regarding the mysterious, magical, and ultimately pseudo-religious nature of Darwinian groupthink and claims. Their mythology is unparalleled for its spectacular imaginings. To paraphrase Axe, we're not dealing with anything close to good science, but with an incoherently dark and demeaning kind of religion. Many evolutionary scientists today are not unlike ancient pagan priests with their secret knowledge, pretending to know and understand what is otherwise unintelligible to the rest of us. Yes, unintelligible is the most fitting word here. And no, the Darwinian priesthood do not understand their theory either. Nor can they offer a coherent defense of it. As world-famous organic chemist and nanoscientist Ph.D. James Tour has stated, no scientist that he has spoken to "understands macroevolution and that includes Nobel Prize winners!"[8]

## A Secular-Cult-Belief

If one does much reading in this area it becomes readily apparent that the core issue with Darwinian evolution has very little to do with empiricism, and everything to do with philosophy. Science has never been the enemy of Christianity, but pseudo-science always will be. Macroevolution is the worst kind of agenda-consensus science. This is not, as frequently and naively declared, a battle between science and religion. This is *all* about faith; an alarming and dangerous kind of secular cult belief from the Darwinian perspective. It is, in the final analysis, a blind faith. There are no data, facts, or proof, just myriad anecdotes, hunches, and guesswork tied together with some imaginative storytelling. "Speculation squared" as someone, somewhere said. Or, as Darwin himself wrote, one's "imagination must fill up very wide blanks."[9] Wells sums it up nicely: "It seems never in the field of science have so many based so much on so little."[10]

The evolution debate is *all* about worldview. Most frequently, this plays out as a clash between theism and atheism, and please understand this: there are eminent scientists on both sides of that question. Accomplished and acclaimed scientists both believe in God and deny Him. Evidencing the fact that Nobel-level science does not preclude the God hypothesis as is often alleged. Parenthetically, God and science are not the same kind of explanation. God explains agency; science explains mechanism. So, any demand to choose between the two as mutually exclusive is always a false choice. God invented science! It's true, modern science isn't burying God; it's burying atheism—as you will read in the subsequent chapters. Close parentheses.

## A Patchwork Thesis

And yes, I know, there are those who hold to a generally unexamined middle ground position regarding macroevolution—a grossly disfigured notion called theistic evolution. Does anyone on either side of the debate not believe it is a blatantly obvious compromise of convenience for the intellectually insecure? Theistic evolution is an untenable patchwork thesis that is wholly incredible to both Darwinists and Bible-believers, betraying a rather determined ignorance of both science and Scripture. You simply cannot read Darwinism into the Genesis text. It doesn't fit texturally, theologically, or even anthropologically. It is the worst kind of exegetical malpractice. Consequently, I will give theistic evolution no further ink. Some things are false whether you disbelieve them or not. Please, take your pick: pseudo-science or God's Word. But don't insult our intelligence.

## A Cosmic Authority Problem

As mentioned in the introduction, the paradigm often encountered in the context of modern science is that of naturalism, or, as it is sometimes called, materialism (I will use these terms synonymously). Naturalism is a primitive fifth-century transparently philosophical assertion that matter is the only reality—a kind of sophisticated pantheism. Obviously, naturalism is not a proper statement of science at all. Such a declaration transcends science. Science, as commonly defined, can neither prove, nor disprove, naturalism. Any honest scientist will readily acknowledge that his craft cannot rule out the supernatural realm. Naturalism is a blind, fact-free leap of faith into an unnatural kind of gloom. A commitment to naturalism is not needed to do science. It is, in fact, excess baggage. There are no good arguments to assert that naturalism is true. There is only personal bias and preference.

Yeah, listen to some of these guys . . .

Philosopher and atheist Thomas Nagel cuts to the chase in a moment of perfect transparency. He writes . . .

> It isn't just that I don't believe in God and, naturally, hope that I'm right in my belief. It's that I hope there is no God! I don't want there to be a God; I don't want the universe to be like that. . . . My guess is that this cosmic authority problem is not a rare condition and that it is responsible for much of the scientism and reductionism of our time. One of the tendencies it supports is the ludicrous overuse of evolutionary biology to explain everything about life . . . .[11]

By the way, scientism and reductionism discard anything that cannot be reduced to the physical. It holds that science is the only way to truth and can ultimately explain everything within the human experience. Obviously, it's a very unscientific assertion. It's religion in a lab-coat.

Geneticist, Richard Lewontin candidly writes . . .

> Our willingness to accept scientific claims that are against common sense is the key to an understanding of the real struggle between science and the supernatural. We take the side of science in spite of the patent absurdity of some of its constructs . . . because we have a prior commitment . . . to materialism. It is not that the methods and institutions of science somehow compel us to accept a material explanation of the phenomenal world but, on the contrary, that we are forced by our [prior commitment] to material causes to create an apparatus of investigation . . . that produce material explanations, no matter how counterintuitive, no matter how mystifying. . . . Moreover, that materialism is absolute, for we cannot allow a Divine foot in the door.[12]

Zoologist D. M. S. Watson reveals that evolution . . .

> is accepted by zoologists, not because it is observed to occur or . . . can be proved by logically coherent evidence to be true, but because the only alternative, special creation, is clearly incredible.[13]

Cosmologist, Paul Davies bluntly states . . .

> Many scientists who are struggling to construct a fully comprehensive theory of the physical universe openly admit that part of the motivation is to finally get rid of God, whom they view as a dangerous and infantile delu-

sion. And not only God, but any vestige of God-talk, such as "meaning" or "purpose" or "design" in nature.[14]

To paraphrase Nagel, many in the scientific community clearly have a significant cosmic authority problem. Ph.D. Donald Batten comments that "[t]he desire to get rid of the Creator-God is a deep seated human trait. . . ."[15] So we see! Apparently, even at the expense of rationality, logic, reason, consistency, coherence, sensibleness, soundness, intelligibility, and just good old-fashioned common sense. I'm not a scientist, but I would think a theory that actually explained the world, and our existence in it, would be preferable to one that does not.

## Practically Magic, Practically Everywhere, Practically All the Time

It is also important to note that in the atheistic, evolutionary model, miracles simply become the order of the day—mind you, with no One around to perform them. Unaccounted for and inexplicable wonders could not fail to occur with breathtaking regularity and in unquantifiable numbers. These are needed to explain, say, a seemingly infinite, finely tuned, mathematically coherent cosmos, as well as the sheer incomprehensible reality of the human mind! Oh, and of course, everything in between! For the adherent of scientism, origins are practically magic, practically everywhere, practically all the time!

Have I already used the word fairy tales? Forgive me if I have, but you know, it just *so* fits. "The word evolution is a wand to wave over mysteries,"[16] Ph.D. Michael Behe colorfully asserts. Regarding the relentless fervor of naturalists to either ignore or explain away the obvious fingerprints of the Creator evident within His creation, Ph.D. David Berlinski writes that this behavior "represents a conspicuous willingness to look anywhere for miracles save in the place they are generally found."[17]

## Predetermined Conclusions

As we've seen, materialists do not discover their materialism *in* the science. They bring it with them *to* the science. Their conclusions are predetermined. They are baked into their presuppositional cake. In assuming Darwin, they think they find Darwin and believe they have proved Darwin. Physicist C. F. von Weizsacker noted, "It is not by its conclusions but by its methodological starting point"[18] that modern science excludes direct creation. Yes, of course we understand that there are facts, but what the man on the street is not often told is that there are various and diverse interpretations of those facts. Only the zealot and the naïve ignore this undeniable certainty regarding evolutionary science. All human beings bring their own unique set of biases and prejudices to every last detail of life. This is true in all forms of human endeavor including religion, politics, journalism, education, business, and yes, the hallowed enterprise of science. It's good counsel from Axe here, and I'm paraphrasing: Trust science on the counting of moons and protons but where interpretation is required, better double check the data.[19]

## Facts Do Not Speak for Themselves

It's not commonly understood that all science is not the same. Experimental sciences such as chemistry and physics differ greatly from the historical sciences such as geology, evolutionary biology, and paleontology. Two parts hydrogen and one part oxygen are always water—no controversy there. But if you're a high profile, grant-seeking, peer-reviewed and published evolutionary biologist and you find part of an unusual jaw bone and a curious looking femur in a dig in Africa, do you have a transitional form or not? Well, of course, it all depends on whom you ask. It depends on what lens the scientist and his consultant are looking through. If they hold a materialistic worldview, they're quite naturally looking for confirmation of that bias, invariably assuming what they desire to find and prove. This never doesn't happen.

Regarding the historical sciences, evolutionary biologist Stephan J. Gould insightfully wrote, "Facts do not 'speak for themselves'; they are read in the light of theory."[20] Science is done by human beings and therein lies a formidable problem for the discipline. Obviously, the essence of true science is to follow the evidence wherever it leads. In biology, this does not happen as often as one might hope. And, oh yes, peer pressure and professional aspirations affect the scientist just like these factors do in every other field of human undertaking. Human nature is always the wild card in the process. Brace yourself. The completely independent, unbiased, unprejudiced, agenda-free, dispassionate scientist is truly a science fiction. Such a creature has yet to be conceived.

Axe writes, "The real problem for science, however, is not people having agendas (as they always do) but rather the institutionalization of agendas [leading to] active suppression of dissent."[21] Regrettably, this is where American academia is with regard to evolution. Authoritarian science reigns. It is holy. It is sacrosanct. Time, chance, and natural selection are the unholy trinity of this secular religion. It is the unquestioned orthodoxy of the day propagated and protected by its priests and adherents while, remarkably, never being fully understood by either. One thing is sure: all heretics and infidels must be mercilessly mocked, discredited, and marginalized. Never mind that there might be valid, pertinent, empirical data accompanied by a rational, logical, intuitively satisfying inference. Nope, can't let facts and sound reasoning frustrate one's Darwinian devotion. Ph.Ds Jerry Fodor and Massimo Piattelli-Palmarini got it right: "Darwinism is scientistic, not scientific."[22]

## That's All You've Got?

We've all heard the grandiose claims of this amateur faith known as scientism. With earnest enthusiasm we've been assured that time, random variation, and natural selection can do every last thing necessary to create, yeah, you. Yes, it is a breathtaking contention. And when we politely request to see the evidence, we are told stories. We are told that some simple cell *emerged* (no one knows exactly what this word means in this context or how such a thing could ever be possible) somehow from somewhere from something for some unknown reason and by some phantom process. And ultimately, by the wholly incomprehensible powers of "evolution," here we are—the "particles to people"[23] saga. Whoa!

Hey, that's a remarkable story. As Lewis noted, it's on par with some of the best mythology he'd ever read. We all like a good story but, seriously, this is all you've got—a couple of fossils, a bone fragment or two, and a yarn devoid of any particulars tying it all together? Really, that's it? Where does one even begin when refuting such fairylike tales? Those irreverent enough to dare object to this in-vogue narrative are quickly put in their place by the high priests of materialism. Dr. Peter Venkman, of *Ghostbusters* fame, could not have articulated the typical elitist condescension any better as he admonished the layman who questioned his methodology. Venkman countered, "Back off man, I'm a scientist!"[24] Isn't a perfect quote a beautiful thing to behold? And from such an esteemed practitioner—a Ghostbuster! Sorry, but it seems to me, it's a discipline not at all unlike evolutionary biology!

## Believing the First Page of the Bible

Some years ago, I preached a sermon series on the opening chapters of Genesis and I skewered the Darwinian faith. After one of the messages, a well-meaning man approached me and said, "What difference does it make? Why fight on this hill? Why challenge accepted science? Why not spend your time preaching the gospel?" There is much to say here that must go unsaid for the sake of brevity. But at the end of the day, truth matters. God's Word matters. Genesis chapters one and two matter. Why should we accommodate the laughable lie? Why should we give any credence to the absurd? Why should we not challenge their dark mythologies? Yes, of course, as Bible-believing Christians we must!

Suffice to say that Biblical Theology comes unwound if one mythologizes the creation account. And what was true for Ph.D. John Cimbala is true for most. He writes, "It wasn't until I could believe the first page of the Bible that I could believe the rest of it."[25] Twentieth-century Christian theologian Francis Schafer reminded us why Genesis matters as he brilliantly wrote . . .

> It is either not knowing or denying the createdness of things that is at the root of the blackness of modern man's difficulties. Give up creation as space-time, historic reality, and all that is left is what Simone Weil called "uncreatedness." It is not that something does not exist, but that it just stands there, autonomous to itself, without solutions and without answers.[26]

## The Fruits of "Uncreatedness"

And what are the consequences of denying *createdness*? Berlinski is right: "Although the horrors of the twentieth century came as a shock, they did not come as a surprise."[27] The unparalleled mass murder of the last century is a testament to the inevitable fruits of *uncreatedness*. It's just where Darwinian naturalism inevitably takes its radical adherents. You can draw a straight line from *On the Origin of Species* to the genocides of Hitler, Stalin, and Mao, who were, along with many others in the previous century, the self-appointed mediators of natural selection—helping evolution along by weeding out the weak and undesirable. On the atheistic, evolutionary worldview there is, as Leo Alexander writes, "such a thing as life not worthy to be lived."[28] And as for the twenty-first century and beyond, Axe warns . . .

> Contemplate the dystopian vision of a generation of human beings believing in their hearts that they are nothing more than bestial accidents fending for themselves in a

> world where morality is fiction and you begin to grasp the true stakes. . . . Heroes are badly needed here. . . .[29]

## What Sons of Light Do

Yeah, heroes are needed! If you're a Christian, you're supposed to be one! It's what "sons of light"[30] do. We boldly push back the darkness as we oppose that which is "falsely called knowledge."[31] Joseph Goebbels and Valdimir Lenin understood that the relentlessly repeated lie effectively becomes the truth. Today, for many, the Darwinian lie has become reality. But I submit that every thinking person intuitively knows better. Again, as George Orwell reputedly said, "During times of universal deceit, telling the truth becomes a revolutionary act." And just to remind you, that's where you and I come in. Real Christians are the ultimate insurgents in this fallen world. We are "strangers and exiles on the earth"[32] reminding everyone who will listen that cutting-edge science is corroborating the visceral instincts and transcendent good news of that ancient warrior king: "Everything says, 'Glory!'"

* * *

"Beware of false knowledge; it is more dangerous than ignorance."[33]
*George Bernard Shaw, Nobel Prize Winning Author and Playwright*

# Notes: Chapter 1

[1] C.S. Lewis, *Christian Reflections* (Grand Rapids, MI: Wm. B. Eerdmands, 1975), 89.
[2] Cited in John Blanchard, *Does God Believe in Atheists?* (Darlington, UK: Evangelical Press, 2000), 116.
[3] R. W. Clark, *The Life of Ernst Chain* (London England: Weidenfeld & Nicolson, 1985), 146-148.
[4] Douglas Axe, *Undeniable* (New York, NY: Harper One, 2016), 217.
[5] Peter Hitchens, *Rage Against God* (Grand Rapids, MI: Zondervan, 2010), 48.
[6] Jonathan Wells, *Icons of Evolution* (Washington D.C.: Regnery Publishing, 2002), xii.
[7] Baumgardner, John R. "Geophysics." In *In Six Days: Why Fifty Scientist Choose to Believe in Creation*, 230. Green Forest, AR: Master Books, 2001.
[8] "A world-famous chemist tells the truth: there's *no* scientist alive today who understands macroevolution" accessed July 24, 2018, https://uncommondescent.com/intelligent-design/a-world-famous-chemist-tells-the-truth-theres-no-scientist-alive-today-who-understands-macroevolution/
[9] Cited in Michael Denton, *Evolution: A Theory in Crisis* (Chevy Chase, MD: Adler & Adler Publishing, 1986), 103.
[10] Wells, 226.
[11] Thomas Nagel, *The Last Word* (Oxford: Oxford University Press, 1997), 130-131.
[12] Richard Lewontin, New York Review of Books, 9 January 1997.
[13] Cited in John Lennox, *God's Undertaker* (Oxford, England: Lion Books, 2009), 97.
[14] Paul Davies, *The Goldilocks Enigma* (Great Britain: Penguin Press, 2016), 15.
[15] Donald Batten, "Natural Selection," in *Evolution's Achilles' Heels* (Powder Springs, GA: Creation Book Publishers, 2014), 24.
[16] Michael Behe, *Darwin's Black Box* (New York, NY: Touchstone, 1998), 181.
[17] David Berlinski, *The Deniable Darwin* (Seattle, WA: Discovery Institute Press, 2009), 460.
[18] Cited in David Berlinski, *The Devil's Delusion* (New York, NY: Basic Books, 2008), 60.
[19] Axe, 38.
[20] Stephen J. Gould, *Ever Since Darwin* (New York, NY: W. W. Norton, 1977) 161-162.
[21] Axe, 54.
[22] Jerry Fodor and Massimo Piattelli-Palmarini, *The Limits of Darwinism New Scientist* 205, no. 2746 (2010): 28-31.
[23] Jonathan Sarfati, *The Greatest Hoax on Earth* (Atlanta, GA: Creation Book Publishers, 2010), 9.
[24] *Ghostbusters*, Produced by Ivan Reitman. Directed by Ivan Reitman.
[25] Cimbala, John M. "Mechanical Engineering." In *In Six Days: Why Fifty Scientist Choose to Believe in Creation*, 201. Green Forest, AR: Master Books, 2001.
[26] Francis Schaeffer, *Genesis in Space and Time* (Downers Grove, IL: InterVarsity, 1972), 30.
[27] Berlinski, *The Devil's Delusion*, 19.

[28] Cited in David Catchpoole and Mark Harwood, "Ethics and Morality," in *Evolution's Achilles' Heels*, 252.
[29] Axe, 55.
[30] 1 Thessalonians 5:5.
[31] 1 Timothy 6:20.
[32] Hebrews 11:13.
[33] Bernard Shaw, *Man and Superman*, a Comedy and a Philosophy (Baltimore, MD: Penguin, 1903).

# ~two~

## Unicorns, Leprechauns, & Quantum Fluctuations

"We have now sunk to a new depth at which restatement of the obvious is the first duty of intelligent men."[1]

*George Orwell, English Novelist, Journalist*

"Once something is thought to come from nothing, something has to give. What gives is logic."[2]

*R. C. Sproul, Ph.D., Christian Author, Theologian*

". . . the Big Bang itself remains outside any causal scheme. . . . The whole vast imposing structure organizes itself from absolutely nothing. This is not simply difficult to grasp. It is incomprehensible."[3]

*David Berlinski, Ph.D., Philosopher, Mathematician*

"In the minds of the brightest men often resides the corner of a fool."[4]

*Aristotle, Ancient Greek Philosopher, Scientist*

Sorry, I know the title might seem somewhat condescending but, hey, that's not really my fault. It's just too easy. As Orwell, Sproul, Berlinski, and Aristotle note, some assertions are just asking for it. Right? Unicorns, leprechauns, and finely-tuned-universe-producing-quantum-fluctuations all have at least one thing in common. They're all just whimsical stories, as far as we know. I did spend seven amazing days in Ireland some years ago but did not encounter one single elf. Nor, unfortunately, had any of the locals I spoke with. It was disappointing, but not unexpected. Turns out, fiction is, well, always fictitious.

While a magical universe is convenient for those who are troubled by the inherent implications of an adequate First Cause, it does, however, leave the same taste in one's mouth as the latest Sasquatch sighting. Make-believe is always fun but it's a less than convincing platform upon which to construct a credible worldview. I thought the Big Bang was science. Turns out, it's a whole lot more like Alice in Wonderland, "believing in impossible things"[5] and all that.

## Bias Is Always Lurking

Cosmology studies the origin and development of the universe. Only a few short decades ago the discipline was "largely viewed as somewhere out there between philosophy and metaphysics."[6] It must be acknowledged that cosmology is, as physicist and M.I.T. professor Max Tegmark states, "not so much about empirical science but about a philosophy—a worldview."[7] It's crucial to understand what cosmologist George F. R. Ellis reveals. He writes, ". . . we are using philosophical criteria in choosing our models. A lot of cosmology tries to hide that."[8] As noted in the last chapter, every scientist on the planet is bringing his worldview to his science. If the cosmologist is a materialist, he will, of course, be interpreting the data through that lens. In an historical science like cosmology, no evidence stands alone. It will be interpreted. Consequently, let the buyer beware. Bias undoubtedly lurks at the back of every origin-of-the-cosmos theorem.

## The Mind Boggles

As many readers already know, current cosmology suggests that the cosmos burst into existence from nothing about 14 billion years ago. It was mockingly called the Big Bang by astronomer Fred Hoyle, and the label stuck. So, where to begin? Maybe, as Sproul advocates, a bit of sophomore logic. The dictionary tells me that logic means "valid reasoning, especially as distinguished from invalid or irrational argumentation."[9] Valid is defined as "well-grounded, sound."[10] Obviously, we have colossal difficulties with the standard scientific Big Bang hypothesis right out of the gate. It runs afoul of the elementary principles of logic. Seriously? Everything from nothing? We all instinctively understand we have no small problem with this line of "invalid and irrational argumentation."

Just listen to some who hold this worldview . . .

- "One physicist writes, 'One thing is clear, in our framing of the questions such as "How did the Universe get started?" is that the Universe was self-creating . . . the Universe was emergent . . . probably derived from an indeterminate sea of potentiality that we call the quantum vacuum. . . .'"[11]
- "Oxford chemist Peter Atkins believes that 'space-time generates its own dust in the process of its own self-assembly.' Atkins dubs this the Cosmic Bootstrap principle, referring to the self-contradictory idea of a person lifting himself up pulling his own bootlaces."[12]

- Science writer Bill Bryson writes, "It seems impossible that you can get something from nothing, but the fact that once there was nothing and now there is a universe is evident proof that you can."[13]
- ". . . atheist Quentin Smith concluded . . . the most reasonable belief is that we came from nothing, by nothing, and for nothing."[14]
- Professor Edward Tryon said, "I offer the modest proposal that our universe is simply one of those things which happen from time to time."[15]

And, as quoted in the introduction, even Stephen Hawking heartily engages in violating the principles of logic in writing about spontaneous creation in his book *The Grand Design*. Ph.D. John Lennox lampoons Hawking's position beautifully.

> What does Hawking mean by spontaneous creation? Hawking's statement seems to be saying: There is something rather than nothing because there is something—and that something comes about spontaneously without any cause or reason except, maybe, that it is possible and just happens.[16]

No, it's not just you. Indeed, the thinking person's mind boggles!

### Science, Logic, and Reason Point to Genesis 1:1

Of course, when physicists talk about nothing, they don't really mean nothing. They mean something that they call nothing. Their nothing is a quantum vacuum which is, of course, not nothing. It's definitely something. Granted, a finely-tuned-universe-producing quantum vacuum is something more like a unicorn than a scientific reality, but still, it's an assertion that something does in fact exist. The question, of course, must be, where did the quantum vacuum come from and just why did that sucker fluctuate? Lennox nails it yet again. He writes, " . . . saying that the universe arises from a fluctuation in a quantum vacuum simply pushes the origins questions one step further back, to asking about the provenance (origin) of the quantum vacuum."[17]

In keeping with Dr. Lennox's unavoidable query, let's return to simple logic. Regarding the origin of the cosmos, among properly caffeinated scientists, philosophers, and theologians, there are only four ideas put forth. *One,* the cosmos is an illusion. Yes, that's philosophical idiocy. *Two,* it is self-created. Yes, that's logically impossible. *Three,* it is eternal. Widely believed and tenaciously held for millennia until the twentieth century when scientific data for a beginning were both theoretically and observationally inferred—making it, as Berlinski writes, "irresistible, inescapable, [and] anchored into fact."[18] It is conclusive. The universe is not eternal. It did begin to exist. And *four,* the cosmos was created by something or Someone that is self-existent. Sound familiar? Yeah, don't you love it when science, logic, and reason all perfectly align pointing inescapably at the Genesis 1:1 scenario?

## Yahweh—The Uncaused Cause

I think we're all on the same page here but let me sum up. It is a universal constant and logical dictate that it's impossible for something to come from nothing. As it has often been said, just as no man can be his own father, no effect can be its own cause. The well-known "kalam cosmological argument" rooted in Biblical Theology, makes an irrefutable case as follows: "Whatever begins to exist has a cause. The universe began to exist. Therefore, the universe has a cause." Twenty-first-century science affirms that the universe began to exist. Therefore, it must have a cause. Not just any cause, but an adequate one. Christians know His name—Jesus Christ.

One of the principal assertions of militant atheist Richard Dawkins in his stunningly superficial book, *The God Delusion,* is that if the universe demands an adequate cause, and God is our answer, then what caused God? Interesting, isn't it? That while atheists were good with an eternal cosmos as pre-twentieth-century cosmology prescribed, they gag on the prospects of an eternal Creator. The "kalam argument" carefully asserts that, "whatever begins to exist has a cause." Bible believers don't believe in a beginning-to-exist god. I'm pretty sure I remember Lennox telling Dawkins in a debate that he "didn't believe in the god Dawkins didn't believe in either," namely, a created or caused god. The Biblical God never began to exist. Yahweh is "I AM, from everlasting to everlasting, the Alpha and the Omega, the first and the last, the beginning and the end."[19] He is the uncaused Cause, the incomparable Uncreated, and the inimitable Unbegun.

While the purely materialistic aspects of the Big Bang hypothesis are logically incoherent, the thesis does have a familiar ring to it, doesn't it? Yes, again, it sounds suspiciously like the creation account found in the Hebrew Scriptures. Science has only recently confirmed what the Bible has been saying all along about the origin of the universe. And without question, evidence-based science is discovering the same to be true regarding the origin of man. It's all that "unaccounted for" code in our DNA. But more on that later. The good news is that the Big Bang establishes the Bible-believer's Genesis 1:1 point. While the poor unbelieving physicist can only speculate about phantom fluctuations within a theorized quantum vacuum, the Christian beholds and worships an omnipotent, genius Creator-God! Again, "Science done right points to God!"[20]

## Serious Trauma

History tells us that the scientific establishment strongly resisted the idea of a universe with a beginning. Aristotle's view of an eternal, or steady state universe that had long held sway, was only reluctantly discarded. It's a fact: in the materialistic clique, the Big Bang gave rise to some serious trauma. Why? One guess is all you'll need. Because, as Berlinski writes, "the Big Bang singularity strikes an uncomfortably theistic note"[21] From his exceptional book entitled, *The Case for a Creator*, Lee Strobel crafts a brilliant paragraph regarding the anxiety the Big Bang hypothesis generated in some circles:

> Einstein admitted the idea of the expanding universe "irritates me."(presumably, said one prominent scientist, "because of its theological implications"). British astronomer Arthur Eddington called it "repugnant." MIT's Philip Morrison said, "I would like to reject it." [Astronomer Robert] Jastrow said it was "distasteful to the scientific mind," adding: "There is a kind of religion in science; it is the religion of a person who believes . . . there is no First Cause. . . . This religious faith of the scientist is violated by the discovery that the world had a beginning under conditions in which the known laws of physics are not valid and as a product of forces or circumstances we cannot discover. When that happens, the scientist has lost control. If he really examined the implications, he would be traumatized.[22]

Yeah, trauma for those afraid of the "light,"[23] awe, wonder, and worship for those who love Him! Five centuries ago, science was sometimes resisted for seeming to cast doubt on the existence of God. Today, empirical science is regularly resisted for its bothersome tendency of bringing a Creator into sharp relief. This, by the way, is happening with increasing frequency across multiple disciplines of modern science, as we will continue to see throughout this book.

## Inference to the Best Explanation

Yes, it's true, science cannot categorically prove or disprove God. But science is seldom about absolute proof, particularly as it relates to the historical sciences such as cosmology. It's always about inference using what is called abductive reasoning, that is, inferring "unseen facts, events, or causes in the past from clues or facts in the present."[24] Such hypotheses "can be firmly established if it can be shown that it represents the best or only explanation of the 'manifest effects' in question . . . philosophers of science call this the method of 'inference to the best explanation'."[25] The "manifest effect" in question is a seemingly infinite, finely-tuned universe capable of supporting life. It is reasonable to ask, what is the best explanation for this effect? There is only One. High-profile, agnostic, astronomer and physicist Robert Jastrow posed the question "Have Astronomers Found God?"[26] His conclusion: ". . . the astronomical evidence points to a theistic view of the origin of the world."[27] Of course, Moses said it much better 3,500 years ago!

Just another prominent scientist or two who concur with the Old Testament Prophet . . .

- Ph.D. astronomer Allen Sandage proposed "that the Big Bang could only be understood as 'a miracle' in which some higher force must have played a role"[28]
- Fellow of the Royal Society astronomer Fred Hoyle observed, "A commonsense interpretation of the facts suggests that a super intellect has monkeyed with the physics, as well as the chemistry and biology . . . ."[29]
- Ph.D. quantum chemist Henry F. Schaeffer III states, "A Creator must exist. The Big Bang ripples and subsequent scientific findings are clearly pointing to an ex nihilo creation consistent with the first few verses of the book of Genesis."[30]
- Nobel Prize-winning physicist Charles Townes writes, "In my view, the question of origin seems to be left unanswered if we explore it from a scientific point of view. Thus, I believe there is a need for some religious or metaphysical explanation. I believe in the concept of God and in his existence."[31]

- ❖ Nobel Prize-winning physicist Arno Penzias commented that "The best data we have are exactly what I would have predicted, had I nothing to go on but the five Books of Moses, the Psalms and the Bible as a whole."[32]

## Every Day Is a Miracle in the Goldilocks Zone

The more science peels back the enigmatic realities of this astonishingly immense, beautiful, complex, and meticulously precise cosmos, the more the God-hypothesis is found to be necessary. God is not only the best explanation; He is the only explanation. Evidenced-based science inescapably points at an omnipotent and omniscient Creator. The question is often posed: Are there miracles? Someone somewhere answered the query perfectly: "It is before our eyes." Christian, life on this small, beautiful, blue planet, circling a 27-million-degree Fahrenheit ball of nuclear fusion at 67,000 miles per hour, in a solar system moving at 500,000 miles per hour around the Milky Way, on a knife's edge of inhabitability in what is otherwise a cold, barren, harsh, hostile, lethal universe, is every day a miracle! Every day you roll out of bed, you're living in a miracle! And you thought it was just another Monday.

Let's flesh out part of that miracle for a moment, that "knife's edge." It's what I've been referring to as I describe the universe as being "fine-tuned." Noted physicist and cosmologist Paul Davies characterizes this phenomenon perfectly with the title of his book *The Goldilocks Enigma: Why Is the Universe Just Right for Life?* The earth is in a Goldilocks zone, not too hot, not too cold. In reading Davies' book, I had two epiphanies. One, I was overcome with a new appreciation for just how smart God is, repeatedly finding myself caught up in worship. And two, I realized, even the most advanced physicists are little more than cavemen hacking away at the data with stone axes. There is a large number of exotic, cosmological theories on the table, but we *know* next to nothing. Davies writes that one must draw "clear distinctions between secure facts, reasonable theorizing and wild conjecture."[33] Good counsel. For it appears, to this layman, that wild conjecture is epidemic in the field.

## An Exquisite Choreography

The not too hot, not too cold thing, meaning, of course, the earth's surface temperature—is only one of many and likely myriad physical and cosmological realities. All of these are exquisitely choreographed to provide the razor-thin possibility of life on our planet. Davies counts twenty such parameters in particle physics and ten more in cosmology. Examples of these would include the following: the cosmological constant or energy density of space; the initial expansion of the Big Bang; the force of gravity; the mass differential between neutrons and protons; entropy; the electromagnetic force; the strong nuclear force; the weak nuclear force; the Earth-Sun relationship; the Earth-moon relationship; Earth's tilt and rotation; the galactic position of Earth; the Earth being protected by gas giant planets; Earth's plate tectonics; the Earth's water-to-land ratio; the Earth's atmosphere, mass, structure, and composition; and the Earth's water, oxygen, carbon, cycles, etc., etc., etc.

Some of these parameters, Davies writes, "must be fined-tuned to an accuracy of less than 1 percent to make the universe fit for life."[34] In attempting to assign a probability for the chance or unintentional fine-tuning of all the necessary physical and environmental factors, physicist and Fellow of the Royal Society Roger Penrose concluded . . .

> That if we jointly considered all the laws of nature that must be fine-tuned, we would be unable to write down such an enormous number because the necessary digits would be greater than the number of elementary particles in the universe.[35]

In other words, the life-sustaining cosmos is no accident. To quote Davies again: "Scientists are slowly waking up to the inconvenient truth—the universe looks suspiciously like a fix."[36] Hoyle agrees, "The universe looks like a put-up job."[37] There is either a hysterically preposterous number of "happy coincidences"[38] defying all possible cosmic odds to a shockingly absurd degree; or God is there! And He is a Genius-Physicist-Creator!

## A Speculation Too Far

So how do dogmatic materialists deal with the "apparent miracle"[39] of an otherwise inhospitable universe producing a perfectly calibrated, bio-friendly planet? Their hypothesis is called the "multi-verse." And yes, we're back to unicorns and leprechauns. The multi-verse postulates up to an infinite number of possible universes. Therefore, it is no shock that at least one universe is just like ours, able to support life. For the unyielding ideologue it seems, as Berlinski notes, "better to have many worlds than one God."[40]

I don't mention this fantastic conjecture because it has any merit but because it is often mentioned as a rebuttal to the hard-science, fine-tuning reality of our planet. Of the multi-verse, Penrose says, "It's an excuse for not having a good theory."[41] And from Davies again, just a quick summary of thoughts from the scientific community on the multi-verse, he writes . . .

> . . . it is . . . a huge departure from the way we normally do science, fallacious reasoning, a speculation too far, an act of faith, a fantasy, intellectually bankrupt, a cheap way out, not science, requires an infinite amount of unverifiable information, a package of wonders, a last resort of the desperate atheist.[42]

Writer Gregg Easterbrook quantifies nicely: "The multi-verse idea rests on assumptions that would be laughed out of town if they came from a religious text."[43] Amen!

Obviously, the desperate attempt to explain away the "apparent miracle"[44] of a perfectly arranged habitat for human life on planet earth via the theorized multi-verse in no way successfully precludes the existence of God. Ph.D. philosopher Alvin Plantinga writes . . .

> . . . if every possible universe exists, then there must be a universe in which God exists, since his existence is logically possible. It then follows that since God is omnipotent and omnipresent he must exist in every universe; hence there is only one universe, this universe, of which he is the Creator and upholder![45]

## Turning Atheists into Theists

Plantinga is right. In examining the cosmos and our existence in it, the open, logical, rational mind is irresistibly drawn to the conclusion that our Creator is there, and He is awesome! Astrophysicist George Greenstein comments . . .

> As we survey all the evidence, the thought insistently arises that some supernatural Agency must be involved. Is it possible that suddenly, without intending to, we have stumbled upon scientific proof of the existence of a Supreme Being?[46]

Fellow of the Royal Astronomical Society cosmologist Edward Harrison concludes: "The fine-tuning of the universe provides prima facie evidence of deistic design."[47] Yeah, this fine-tuning stuff has been known to turn atheists into theists. See former atheist Anthony Flew's book, entitled *There Is A God.*

So, in answer to the millennia-old question, why is there something rather than nothing? The Bible tells us, and the data confirms. God created! There was only one Witness to creation. Everything anyone else has to say is pure, unsubstantiated, blind speculation. We would do well to humbly receive His testimony. Neither science nor reason oppose God's Genesis revelation. There is a worship-provoking Mind behind the universe as King David sings, "The heavens are telling of the glory of God and their expanse is declaring the work of His hands. Day to day pours forth speech and night to night reveals knowledge."[48] Yes, every starry night proclaims it: "Everything says, 'Glory!'"

* * *

"... naturalism is on hard times in cosmology; the deeper you get into it, the harder it is to get rid of the God hypothesis. Taken together, the Big Bang and general relativity provide a scientific description of what Christians call creatio ex nihilo—creation out of nothing."[49]
*Stephen C. Meyer, Ph.D. Philosophy of Science*

# Notes: Chapter 2

[1] George Orwell, Review of *Power; A New Social Analysis* by B. Russell in *The Adelphi* (January 1939), 375-377.
[2] R. C. Sproul, *Not A Chance* (Grand Rapids, MI: Baker, 1994), 11.
[3] David Berlinski, *The Deniable Darwin* (Seattle, WA: Discovery Institute Press, 2009), 229.
[4] Cited in Sproul, 16.
[5] Lewis Carroll, *Alice Through the Looking Glass* (London, England: Macmillan, 1871), 84.
[6] Cited in John Hartnett, "Cosmology: Exposing the Big Bang's Fatal Flaws," in *Evolutions Achilles Heels*, (Powder Springs, GA: Creation Books, 2014), 224.
[7] Ibid., 219.
[8] Ibid.
[9] "Logic," *The American Heritage Dictionary* (Boston: Houghton Mifflin Co., 1985).
[10] "Valid," Ibid.
[11] Cited in David Berlinski, *The Devil's Delusion* (New York, NY: Basic Books, 2008), 96.
[12] Cited in John Lennox, *God and Stephen Hawking* (Oxford, England: Lion Hudson, 2014), 31.
[13] Bill Bryson, *A Short History of Nearly Everything* (New York: Broadway, 2003), 13.
[14] Cited in Lee Strobel, *The Case For a Creator* (Grand Rapids, MI: Zondervan, 2004), 99.
[15] Ibid., 100.
[16] Lennox, *God and Stephen Hawking*, 67-68.
[17] Lennox, *God's Undertaker* (Oxford, England; Lion Books, 2009), 69.
[18] Berlinski, *The Devil's Delusion*, 72, 78.
[19] Exodus 3:14, Psalm 90:2, Revelation 22:13.
[20] Steven Meyer, cited in Strobel, 77.
[21] Berlinski, *The Devil's Delusion*, 97.
[22] Strobel, 112.
[23] John 8:12.
[24] Steven C. Meyer, *Signature In The Cell* (New York, NY: HarperCollins Publishers, 2009), 153.
[25] Ibid., 154.
[26] *New York Times*, 25 June 1978.
[27] Ibid.
[28] Gregg Easterbrook, "Academics Ponder the Ties Between Faith and Fact," *Los Angeles Times*, March 14, 1999, 1.
[29] Berlinski, *The Deniable Darwin*, 300.
[30] Cited in Lennox, *God's Undertaker*, 30.
[31] Charles Townes, *Making Waves*, American Physical Society, 1995.
[32] Cited in Strobel, 77.

[33] Paul Davies, *The Goldilocks Enigma* (New York, NY: Houghton Mifflin Harcourt, 2006), xiii.
[34] Ibid., 146.
[35] Roger Penrose, *The Emperor's New Mind* (New York: Oxford, 1989), 344.
[36] Cited in Berlinski, *The Devil's Delusion*, 111.
[37] Ibid., 110.
[38] William Dembski & Sean McDowell, *Understanding Intelligent Design* (Eugene, OR: Harvest House, 2008), 158.
[39] Stephen Hawking, cited in Lennox, *God and Stephen Hawking*, 48.
[40] Berlinski, *The Devil's Delusion*, 135.
[41] Cited in Lennox, *God and Stephen Hawking*, 50.
[42] Davies, 150-265.
[43] Gregg Easterbrook, "The New Convergence" *Wired* (December 2002).
[44] Stephen Hawking, cited in Lennox, *God and Stephen Hawking*, 48.
[45] Cited in Lennox, *God and Stephen Hawking*, 93.
[46] Cited in Strobel, 153.
[47] Edward Harrison, *Masks of the Universe* (New York: Collier, 1985), 263,252.
[48] Psalm 19:1-2.
[49] Cited in Strobel, 77.

# ~three~

## "Fudging & Finagling" the Fossils

"But what is at issue for Darwin's theory is not the fossils that exist but the ones that do not."[1]
*David Berlinski, Ph.D., Philosopher, Mathematician*

"To take a line of fossils and claim that they represent a lineage is not a scientific hypothesis that can be tested, but an assertion that carries the same validity as a bedtime story—amusing, perhaps even instructive, but not scientific."[2]
*Henry Gee, Ph.D., Paleontologist, Evolutionary Biologist*

". . . the public is rarely told that the fossils have been placed into 'preexisting narrative structures' or that the story . . . rests on 'biases, preconceptions and assumptions.'"[3]
*Jonathan Wells, Ph.D. Religious Studies, Molecular Biology*

"In short, if evolution means the gradual change of one kind of organism into another kind, the outstanding characteristic of the fossil record is the absence of evidence for evolution."[4]
*Phillip E. Johnson, Author and Professor of Law, University of California*

To paraphrase the Son of Man, indeed, the rocks will cry out![5] And so they are. The rocks are telling their story. To echo Berlinski, Gee, Wells, and Johnson, it's not the same story the scientific establishment, academia, and the media are selling. The rocks are testifying that the history of life does not reveal a mindless, unintended, unguided, graduated, natural process but rather an ingenious, designed, directed, instantaneous, supernatural, omnipotent, creative act of an Infinite Intellect.

The rocks will not be denied. They will have their say. They've joined in the universal and ever-present chorus of the entire created order. They are quietly shouting what the "stars, beasts, birds, earth, fish, seas, fields, trees, rivers, and mountains"[6] are declaring. Yeah, you guessed it: all of creation joyfully harmonizes with that celebrated Hebrew lyricist, "Everything says, 'Glory'!'"

## A Papered-Over Scientific Fact

Even the guys who study fossils (paleontologists) acknowledge that something's up with the rocks. They're simply not cooperating with the macroevolutionary narrative. In fact, the rocks are unequivocally contradicting that unsuccessful medical student, turned seminarian, turned gentleman naturalist, Charles Darwin.

This may be news to some readers, but the Darwinian hypothesis is in absolute contradiction with the geological record. Of course, you wouldn't know this from reading your average science textbook or by visiting your local museum. But Darwin knew it. He acknowledged it in *On the Origin of Species*. He wrote, "The number of intermediate and transitional links, between all living and extinct species, must have been inconceivably great."[7] And yet, they are not. According to Darwin, these transitional forms must exist in virtually unlimited number. But they are wholly, completely, entirely, totally, altogether, and in every respect absent. Do you get my point in multiplying adverbs here? The intermediate fossils are not there. They are nonexistent. This is no small detail.

Darwin understood the dilemma. He wrote, "Why then is not every geological formation and every stratum full of such intermediate links? Geology assuredly does not reveal any such finely graduated organic chain."[8] He went on to acknowledge that this was, "the most obvious and gravest objection, which can be urged against my theory."[9] He apparently believed future discoveries would ultimately vindicate his model. They haven't. Did I say that intermediate fossils simply do not exist in the geological record? I thought I did but, you know, you can never really say that often enough. Maybe more will hear and grasp the import of this indisputable yet often papered-over scientific fact.

## Paleontologists Behaving Badly

It is, of course, the undying hope of every earnest paleontologist to find the missing link. Or as Darwin made clear, the "inconceivably great number" of missing links, plural, squared, cubed, ad-infinitum. You know, a lot. Johnson said it well, with only a touch of sarcasm: "The problem with the fossil record is how evolution always happened in such a manner as to escape detection."[10] Or as Ph.D. paleontologist Niles Eldredge notes, "Evolution cannot forever be going on somewhere else. Yet that's how the fossil record has struck many a forlorn paleontologist looking to learn something about evolution."[11] The fossil record makes one thing explicitly clear: macroevolution never happens . . . anywhere.

The utter absence of any incontestable transitional forms in the fossil record is, as noted Ph.D. paleontologist Stephen J.

Gould said, "The trade secret of paleontology."[12] And here you thought scientists were always forthright. Sorry to break it to you, but Darwinists are known to be more than a little stealthy when it comes to facts they can't shoehorn into their pet hypothesis. I almost entitled this chapter *Paleontologists Behaving Badly*, for indeed one would expect that adult professionals might, oh, you know, tell the rest of us the truth—that regarding intermediate forms and the fossil record, there's just no there, there.

In his superb book entitled *Does God Believe in Atheists?* John Blanchard exposes the roots and fallacies of materialism. It's a must-read for any serious Christian. Regarding the trade secret of paleontologists, Blanchard pens a wonderful paragraph underscoring their clandestine duplicity with respect to the fossil record:

> Stephen J. Gould, Professor of Geology and Paleontology at Harvard University . . . frankly confesses, "All paleontologists know that the fossil record contains precious little in the way of intermediate forms; transitions between major groups are characteristically abrupt. . . ." In other words, generations of students . . . have had the wool pulled firmly over their eyes! Niles Eldredge confirms the conspiracy: "We paleontologists have said that the history of life supports . . . [the story of gradual adaptive change] . . . all the while knowing that it does not." Evolutionist Jeremy Rifkin has been positively scathing about the attempt to make the fossils speak out in favor of Darwinism: "What the 'record' shows is nearly a century of fudging and finagling by scientists to conform with Darwin's notions, all to no avail. Today the millions of fossils stand as very visible, ever-present reminders of the paltriness of the arguments and the overall shabbiness of the theory that marches under the banner of evolution."[13]

## You've Got to Be Kidding, Right?

Fudging and finagling? You're right; these are not techniques known to engender a high level of confidence. To paraphrase Berlinski, ordinary men and women are suspicious of Darwin's theory . . . [and] these intellectual anxieties are not misplaced.[14] He continues,

> . . . Darwin's theory of evolution remains the only scientific theory to be widely championed by the scientific community and widely disbelieved by everyone else. No matter the effort made by biologists, the thing continues to elicit the same reaction it has always elicited: You've got to be kidding, right?[15]

I confess that's how the so-called evidence and dubious arguments have always landed on me. Seriously?

## The Fall of an Icon

Yes, you remember there is that one iconic fossil that we have all seen in the textbooks. It's known as *Archaeopteryx*. We were told it was one of those elusive missing links between reptiles and birds. Oops, not so much. Most paleontologists today agree with their colleague Ph.D. Larry Martin who writes, "Archaeopteryx is not ancestral of any group of modern birds [instead it is] the earliest known member of a totally extinct group of birds."[16] And yet you may not be surprised to learn that even though it is now known to be a false assertion, "some biology textbooks continue to present Archaeopteryx as the classic example of a missing link."[17] As a side note, presently, one of the prevailing views is that birds evolved from dinosaurs. Yeah, I know. To quote Wells again, "This isn't science. This isn't even myth. This is comic relief."[18]

## The Imaginary Tree of Life

Another famous image from our high school days is that of Darwin's so-called, *Tree of Life*. It's Darwin's own diagram of how he envisioned all of life evolving from one common ancestor. And yes, you guessed it: this image still appears in most textbooks although it is clearly at odds with the geological and fossil records. It's true, Darwin's tree has been uprooted by Darwinian paleontologists. This is, of course, not their aim but is the unavoidable consequence of continuing to dig stuff up. Johnson is right: "... the fossil problem for Darwinism is getting worse all the time." [19] The rocks don't lie. The *Tree* is fiction. Based on the fossil evidence (and the molecular and genetic data), there is no universal ancestor. The fossils are unmistakably pointing to the first two chapters of Genesis instead of *On the Origin of Species*. The geological strata categorically contradict Darwin's *Tree* in several irreconcilable ways.

## Bam!

First, there's that inconvenient yet uncontested fact known as the Cambrian explosion. It simply blasts Darwin's *Tree* back into the pseudo-scientific realm from which it originated. Ph.D. William Dembski and Sean McDowell write, "Prior to the Cambrian explosion, the fossil record consists almost exclusively of single-celled organisms, and then—bam!—the major animal body plans emerge in a geological moment without any transitional intermediate forms."[20] Bam is right! The rocks tell us that abruptly, suddenly, extensively, inexplicably the animals appeared. It's the biological equivalent of the Big Bang. The animals weren't; then they were. For the materialist, writes Wells, "the Cambrian explosion remains a paradox."[21] Yes, true if you revere Darwin; not so much if you revere Jehovah!

## According to Its Kind

Secondly, there's that pesky matter of what science calls stasis in the fossils. Meaning, the animals don't change. Once a creature is identified in the rocks, it just never changes after that. How does Genesis say it over, and over, and over, and over again? All living things procreate and multiply "after their kind."[22] God and the evidence agree yet again! Obviously, this kind of stability and permanence inside animal groups is contrary to Darwin's hypothesis. Minor changes are seen within species, but this is what is known as microevolution which no one denies has, and does, occur. The Cambrian explosion, together with stasis, elucidates why gaps persist at all major breaks in the hypothetical Darwinian lineage. You guessed it. The gaps exist because the transitional creatures never did. The missing links are not missing because they're missing. They're missing because they're imaginary, ". . . simply illusions"[23] in the evolutionists' minds.

## No Intermediate Forms

Ever persistent and unhindered by the overwhelming lack of fossil evidence, the Darwinists have proposed some silly notions such as *punctuated equilibrium* and *abrupt emergence* without really bothering to inform us how either could have possibly ever happened. Both ideas call for sudden and drastic change within a lineage which, of course, contradicts one of the core precepts of Darwinian theory—namely a slow gradualism in the evolution of species. There is simply no known natural mechanism for the kind of rapid evolutionary progress these speculative theories necessitate. Regarding the lack of fossil data to verify macroevolutionary theory, I guess it must be said. The absence of evidence *is* the evidence of absence. In short, the rocks are telling us that macro-Darwinian evolution is a bankrupt hypothesis. It never happened.

And even at this late date, we're still hearing Darwin's own excuse incessantly repeated regarding the so-called gaps in the fossil record. He wrote, "The explanation lies, as I believe, in the extreme imperfection of the geological record."[24] So, is the fossil record deficient? Ph.D. biochemist Michael Denton points out . . .

> . . . that 97.7% of living orders of land vertebrates are represented as fossils, and 79.1% of living families of land vertebrates—87.8% if birds are excluded, as they are less likely to become fossilized.[25]

I'm no statistician, but numbers like 88% to 98% do not sound like a deficient record to me. Is it remotely possible that a disciple of Darwin would ever consider the prospect that what we have here is not a flawed fossil record but a flawed theory?

Additionally, regarding the lack of intermediate forms, Eldridge writes . . .

> This oddity has been attributed to gaps in the fossil record which gradualists expected to fill when rock strata of the proper age had been found. In the last decade, however, geologists have found rock layers of all divisions of the last 500 million years [by conventional dating] and no transitional forms were contained in them.[26]

Moreover, Denton states that Darwin's appeal to an imperfect fossil record is "largely a circular argument because the only significant evidence he was able to provide for its 'extreme imperfection' was the very absence of the intermediates that he sought to explain."[27]

## A Philosophical Prerequisite

So, why do paleontologists tenaciously hold to this fossil-free evolutionary notion? Because they want to. I know that sounds overly dismissive but it's just what it is. For the materialist, the atheist, the agnostic, the insecure academic, and the indoctrinated scientist, there is no other refuge. Darwin is all they have. If there were any alternative naturalistic theories concerning how complex life came to exist on the planet, they would gleefully pile on. For those who are disinclined to embrace God's version of events in Genesis, Darwinian theory, albeit absurd and unsubstantiated, is *the* vital component of their worldview. Macroevolution is a philosophical prerequisite for those who deny a Creator. It cannot not be true. It is demanded by their own self-imposed definitions. And if it must be true, then any evidence (or as we have seen, apparently no evidence) will suffice. As we continue to note, people have always loved a good story, and that is really all Darwin and his minions have proffered.

Concerning this uncompromising evolutionary mindset, Johnson writes . . .

> For them there is no need to test the theory itself, for there is no respectable alternative to test it against . . . Darwinism to them [is] not a theory open to refutation but a fact to be accounted for. . . . The prevailing assumption in evolutionary science seems to be that speculative possibilities, without experimental confirmation, are all that is really necessary.[28]

To the dogmatic, hardnosed materialist, Darwin's theory will never fail to clear every evidentiary hurdle simply because it will never be allowed to. There will always be yet another equivocation of the data or, you know, a little more "fudging and finagling."

## Imagination Must Fill Up Very Wide Blanks

In this regard, Ph.D. geologist Emil Silvestru writes that . . .

> . . . evolution is a worldview that is used to interpret all evidence, no matter what is found. It cannot be falsified by a fossil find. The fossil is simply reinterpreted to make it look like it proves evolution all along.[29]

Johnson adds that, ". . . fossils don't tell their own story . . . the tale of ancestors being modified into descendents still relies on Darwinian theory to fill in 99 percent of the details."[30] As noted in Chapter One, Darwin himself acknowledged that one's own "imagination must fill up the very wide blanks."[31] Again, flights of self-indulgent fancy can certainly be enjoyable but are less than convincing to those of us who would like to see an unembellished fact or two.

Here are just a few more informed views regarding Darwin and the fossil record . . .

- "The fossil record does not convincingly document a single transition from one species to another,"[32] according to Ph.D. paleontologist Steven Stanley.
- Ph.D. John Lennox writes, ". . . the fossil record gives no good examples of macroevolution. This will sound surprising to many people since it is a widespread public impression that one of the most powerful evidences for evolution comes from the fossil record."[33]
- Ph.D. paleontologist Colin Patterson notes, "I will lay it on the line—there is not one such fossil [a fossil which is ancestral or transitional] for which one could make a watertight argument."[34]
- Ph.D. Jonathan Sarfati writes, "Despite claims . . . that perfect missing links have been discovered, the claims evaporate under careful analysis. This includes Archaeopteryx between reptiles and birds, Tiktaalik between fish and land creatures, Pakicetus and Basilosaurus between land mammals and whales. . . . The fossil record overall contradicts evolutionary expectations. . . ."[35]
- Ph.D. biologist Ariel A. Roth states, "Evolution requires intermediate forms between species and paleontology does not provide them."[36]
- Dembski and McDowell write, "Although one would not know this from standard biology textbooks. . . . The fossil record is even more at odds with Darwin's theory now than it was when he first proposed it."[37]

### Young Earth or Old Earth?

To close out our venture into the geological realm, it seems good to include just a word about the age of the earth. Yeah, I have no idea! God does not tell us. Obviously, not being a Hebrew scholar regarding the biblical text or a geologist regarding the rocks, my opinion can be dismissed as easily as the next guy's. But while I hold a young-earth position, I concede that Lennox raises what seems to be a possible qualification when he notes:

> Genesis 1:1 could mean the initial creation did not necessarily take place on day 1 as is frequently assumed. The initial creation took place before day 1, but Genesis does not tell us how long before. This means that the question of the age of the earth . . . is a separate question from the interpretation of the days, a point that is frequently overlooked. . . . It would therefore be logically possible to believe that the days of Genesis are twenty-four-hour days and to believe that the universe is very ancient. . . . Although Scripture could be understood as teaching that the earth is young, it does not have to be interpreted that way. . . . There is a danger of understanding the text as saying less than it does, but also a danger of trying to make it say more.[38]

Unless I'm in error regarding the Hebrew text, the structure of the opening verses of Genesis seem to leave open the possibility that the earth could be quite old. I am not arguing for that. I am simply saying it seems wise to acknowledge Lennox's point. Since God was the only witness to creation, what He says supersedes any other factor, contention, or argument. All we need to do is rightly divide the Word. So, while noting Lennox's line of reasoning as a plausible qualification, I am a young-earth and 24-hour-creation-day guy. If we just let words mean what words mean and apply normal rules of grammar, it's what the Genesis text is saying relative to the creation days. Although prevailing scientific theory takes a radically different view, as prominent theologian John MacArthur aptly writes, "Modern scientific opinion is not a valid hermeneutic for interpreting Genesis. . . . The Bible is supreme truth, and therefore it is the standard by which scientific theory should be evaluated, not vise versa."[39]

If you roll out of bed on a regular basis, you've no doubt been exposed to some of the arguments for an old earth. What are less well known are the intriguing natural phenomena that point to a young earth. There are many. Following is an abbreviated list. If the cosmos and earth are 13.8 and 4.6 billion years old respectively, then . . . [t]he spiral shape of our galaxy would no longer exist, comets would have disintegrated, there would be more supernova remnants, the earths magnetic field would have totally decayed, the moon drift is inadequate, there is not enough dust and meteor debris on the moon's surface, there is too little sodium in the sea and sediment on the sea floor, there is too much helium remaining in minerals, and there is too much carbon 14 in deep geological strata. As Sarfati writes, "far more chronometers [time indicators] point to a young age."[40]

## Notoriously Unreliable

Of course, academia and the media continue to zealously propagate the old-earth narrative supported principally by radiometric dating. Well, radiometric dating is based on a whole lot of speculative, unknowable, and unproven assumptions about the past—and yes, you guessed it, a whole lot of subjective interpretation of the results. Ph.D. botanist George Howe asks the crucial question: "Is there any feature about any dating method that actually satisfies all the ordinary criteria of real science?"[41] It's understood in the profession that radiometric ages are notoriously unreliable. That's how it's possible for lava flows from the twentieth-century eruptions of Mt. St. Helens in North America and Mt. Ngaurahoe in New Zealand to be dated anywhere from 350,000 to 2.8 million years. These are the kinds of margins of error (and greater) we're talking about with these dating techniques. When publishing, one expert admits . . .

> If a C14 date supports our theories, we put it in the main text. If it does not entirely contradict them, we put it in a footnote. And if it is completely "out of date," we just drop it. And if the dates are rejected, the difference can be explained away—the technical term is "interpreted."[42]

Yeah, we're back to "fudging and finagling" yet again.

This is what we know for sure when it comes to the interpretation of the rocks, that "it is impossible to separate theory, presupposition, and assumption from models of geological history."[43] In other words, the individual scientist's worldview inevitably guides and governs the conclusions drawn. Never forget, this always happens in the historical sciences. Long ages are sacrosanct; they are read into the data because they must be. They are necessary for Darwin to be true. Ph.D. Jim Mason writes . . .

> Radiometric dating does not provide the unequivocal support for the millions and billions of years required by evolution. In fact, radiometric dating provides evidence for a much younger earth, in line with the history recorded in the Bible.[44]

Always remember that ". . . the age of the earth can neither be proved or disproved by science . . . such work amounts to a feasibility study, not proof."[45] Remember, too, that "The scientific evidence for long age rests primarily on the selection of evidence favorable to the long-age position rather than to the evaluation of all available evidence."[46]

## A Simpler, More Complete Explanation

And for any readers who are wondering, yes, as Ph.D. Tasman Walker writes, the geological evidence is in keeping with "what we would expect from the Bible's account of the global catastrophic flood of Noah's day."[47] Silvestru adds . . .

> The possibility that all phyla were created by God during the unique event of Creation, drastically tested and filtered through a global flood, is utterly rejected by secular scientists, even though it is a simpler and more complete explanation. When geological and paleontological facts visibly support this explanation, they are subtly made invisible by academia and the media.[48]

As noted earlier, Darwinists not only like to keep secrets; they are always eagerly amenable to the "censorship of dissenting views."[49] As accomplished as the Darwinian dogmatists are in this regard, they cannot censor the clarion declaration of the rocks, for they are indeed shouting with all creation, "Everything says, 'Glory!'"

* * *

"Fossils are fickle. Bones will sing any song you want to hear."[50]
*Jonathan D. Sarfati, Ph.D. Physical Chemistry*

# Notes: Chapter 3

[1] David Berlinski, *The Deniable Darwin* (Seattle, WA: Discovery Institute Press, 2009), 344.
[2] Henry Gee, *In Search of Deep Time* (New York, NY: Free Press, 1999), 23,32, 116-17.
[3] Jonathan Wells, *Icons of Evolution* (Washington D.C.: Regnery Publishing, 2002), 225-226.
[4] Phillip E. Johnson, *Darwin on Trial* (Downers Grove, IL: Intervarsity Press, 2010), 73.
[5] Luke 19:40.
[6] Job 38:7, Job 12:7-10, Psalm 96:11-12, Psalm 98:7-8.
[7] Charles Darwin, *On the Origin of Species* (Cambridge, MA: Harvard University, 1964), 281-282.
[8] Ibid., 280.
[9] Ibid.
[10] Johnson, 76.
[11] Cited in Michael Behe, *Darwin's Black Box* (New York, NY: Touchstone, 1996), 27.
[12] John Lennox, *God's Undertaker* (Oxford, England; Lion Books, 2009), 114.
[13] John Blanchard, *Does God Believe in Atheists?* (Darlington, UK: Evangelical Press, 2000), 107-108.
[14] Berlinski, *The Deniable Darwin*, 110-111.
[15] David Berlinski, *The Devil's Delusion* (New York, NY: Basic Books, 2008), 186.
[16] Cited in Wells, 116.
[17] Wells, 134.
[18] Ibid., 134.
[19] Johnson, 80.
[20] William Dembski & Sean McDowell, *Understanding Intelligent Design* (Eugene, OR: Harvest House, 2008), 71-72.
[21] Wells, 48.
[22] Genesis 1:21, 24, 25.
[23] John R. Baumgardner, "Geophysics," in *In Six Days: Why Fifty Scientist Choose to Believe in Creation,* (Green Forest, AR: Master Books, 2001), 234.
[24] Darwin, 280.
[25] Cited in Jonathan Sarfati, *The Greatest Hoax on Earth* (Atlanta, GA: Creation Book Publishers, 2010), 109.
[26] Cited in Michael Denton, *Evolution: A Theory in Crisis* (Chevy Chase, MD: Adler & Adler Publishing, 1986), 194.
[27] Denton, 57.
[28] Johnson, 49, 60, 65.
[29] Emil Silvestru, "The Fossil Record," in *Evolutions Achilles Heels* (Powder Springs, GA: Creation Books, 2014), 121.
[30] Johnson, 15.

[31] Cited in Denton, 103.
[32] Cited in Johnson, 73.
[33] Lennox, *God's Undertaker*, 113.
[34] Cited in Lennox, *God's Undertaker*,115.
[35] Sarfati, 123, 144.
[36] Ariel A. Roth, "Biology," in *In Six Days*, 93.
[37] Dembski & McDowell, 69.
[38] John Lennox, *Seven Days That Divide The World* (Grand Rapids, MI: Zondervan, 2016), 53.
[39] John MacArthur, *Battle For The Beginning* (Nashville, TN: W Publishing Group, 2001), 22.
[40] Sarfati, 202.
[41] George F. Howe, "Botany," in *In Six Days*, 256.
[42] Cited in Sarfati, 194.
[43] Tasman Walker, "The Geological Record," in In *Evolution's Achilles Heels*, 159.
[44] Jim Mason, "Radiometric Dating," in *Evolution's Achilles Heels*, 213.
[45] Jeremy L. Walter, "Mechanical Engineering," in *In Six Days*, 11.
[46] Kerr C. Thomson, "Geophysics," in *In Six Days*, 222.
[47] Walker, 182.
[48] Silvestru, 128.
[49] Wells, 235.
[50] Sarfati, 138.

# ~four~

## Monkey-Men & Assorted Other Mythologies

"Darwinist evolution is an imaginative story about who we are and where we came from, which is to say it is a creation myth."[1]

*Phillip E. Johnson, Author and Professor of Law, University of California*

"But beyond what we have in common with the apes, we have nothing in common, and while the similarities are interesting, the differences are profound."[2]

*David Berlinski, Ph.D., Philosopher, Mathematician*

"Out of all the major sequences of Darwinian evolution, the evolution of man is the nearest to us in time and should, therefore, be backed by an abundance of fossils. It isn't."[3]

*Emil Silvestru, Ph.D., Geologist*

"The general public is rarely informed of the deep-seated uncertainty about human origins that is reflected in statements by scientific experts. Instead, we are simply fed the latest version of somebody's theory . . . typically . . . illustrated with fanciful drawings of cave men. . . ."[4]

*Jonathan Wells, Ph.D., Religious Studies, Molecular Biology*

It is the worst book I've ever tried to read. It was well intentioned opposition research on my part, but I couldn't finish it. It was wholly bereft of any salvageable merit. Watching the grass grow or taking a nap had decidedly more intellectual appeal than wading through the strikingly inane ramblings of a willfully deceived man. Are atheists utterly oblivious to the fact that all their pretentious critiques of religion quite naturally fold back upon their own materialistic beliefs? Apparently, Richard Dawkins is not so self-aware. In his book *The God Delusion,* it just never seems to occur to him that what he is espousing is, in fact, a dogmatic and entirely faith-based worldview, namely, his militant atheism.

In his book, Dawkins defines the word delusion for us as "a persistent false belief held in the face of strong contradictory evidence . . ."[5] Then he quotes an obscure philosopher who writes, "When one person suffers from a delusion, it is called insanity. When many people suffer from a delusion it is called religion."[6] I'm sure I'm not the only one to notice the painfully obvious irony as Dawkins not only handily indicts himself but a sizable portion of the modern scientific community, academia, and media regarding their passionate and unbending devotion to scientism—the delusional religion of secular man.

It is indeed stunning to see a man with Dawkins' scholarly credentials write, ". . . Darwin made it possible to be an intellectually fulfilled atheist."[7] How can an educated man with even some small fraction of the facts in hand possibly make such a statement? Not only is Darwin's core evolutionary hypothesis unsupported by the data in any pertinent discipline of science, it doesn't even begin to touch such questions as the origin of life from non-life, the genesis of genetic information, and the irreducible complexity of biological systems. With such transparent and yawning deficiencies in evolutionary theory, how can a thinking person talk about intellectual fulfillment? As is often the case, Darwinists seldom let the data get in the way of their dogma. How did Dawkins' philosopher say it? "When many people suffer from a delusion it is called religion."[8] Yeah, we see, Richard, we see—a religion demonstrating a pathological fear of the "Light."[9]

## Selling the Lie

You've seen it in textbooks. You've seen it in museum exhibits. You've seen it on posters, and tee-shirts, and bumper stickers. It's one of the most ubiquitous images of our age: the Darwinian sequence of the late stages of mankind's supposed evolution. From left to right we see a chimplike creature, then a gorillalike creature, then a hominidlike creature, then a cavemanlike creature, and then we see ourselves. It's the iconic evolutionary visual—universally recognized worldwide and, yes, you guessed it, wholly unsupported by the evidence. It is merely conceptual. There is no basis in fact, none. Of course, that is certainly not for lack of funding, or digging, or fanciful storytelling. Every self-respecting Darwinian paleontologist, anthropologist, and biologist is dead set on proving the monkey-man sequence. Following, is a small bit of that sordid history summarized in part from John Blanchard's excellent chapter on the topic, flawlessly entitled, *Impossible Things Before Breakfast*[10] from his splendid book, *Does God Believe in Atheists?*

## Neanderthal Man

In 1857, quarry workers dug up a partial skeleton near Düsseldorf, Germany. Similar remains have also been found in Africa and Asia. These skeletons came to be called Neanderthals and were alleged to be a missing link between ape and man. Oops . . . in 1908, a Neanderthal skeleton was found buried in a suit of armor in a tomb in Poland. Yeah, a missing link ape-man in a suit of armor . . . not going to play well in National Geographic. Consequently, that magazine will likely never bother to tell you about it. Why bother with findings that don't agree with the prescribed evolutionary narrative? Don't want to disquiet the groupthink of their subscribers in any way. Neanderthals are now seen as nothing more than human beings with unusual skeletal features likely caused by rickets, arthritis, or vitamin D deficiencies. While Neanderthals are still in some textbooks and museums represented as a subhuman species, they were, as scholar Marvin Lubenow writes, ". . . a card-carrying member of the human race."[11]

### Java Man

In the early 1890s in Indonesia, over the period of about a year and within a perimeter of fifty feet or so, Eugene Dubois dug up a skull fragment, a thigh-bone, and three teeth. He then announced that he'd found an "upright ape-man" who would come to be called Java Man. Oops . . . twenty-eight years later, Dubois admitted that he had found human skeletal remains in the same geological stratum. Yes, in his initial reporting and for nearly three decades, he failed to mention this important piece of information. Java Man wasn't a missing link after all, just a run-of-the-mill human being. Journalist and author Lee Strobel reveals that as a young man he was captivated by the theorized Java Man narrative but had no idea "the lifelike depiction of Java Man was little more than speculation fueled by evolutionary expectations of what he should have looked like if Darwinism were true."[12] This is what you discover when you read a book or two about macroevolutionary claims. They're always just a lot of over-the-top guesswork, or as guys in lab coats like to call it, interpretation.

### Piltdown Man

In 1912, Charles Dawson showed up at the British Museum with some bones, teeth, and primitive tools found near Piltdown, Sussex. The remains were dated at 500,000 years old and hailed as a missing link. The find was given the name Piltdown Man and hit all the textbooks and museums. The scientists who purported to establish Piltdown as an ape-man transitional received knighthoods and over 500 doctoral dissertations were written about the discovery. Oops . . . Piltdown Man was revealed to be a colossal fraud made up of a human skull and the jawbone of an orangutan whose teeth had been filed to look more human. It must be noted that it took the scientific community decades to admit that Piltdown Man was a hoax. As John Blanchard writes, "All we can say for certain is that Piltdown Man, once hailed as proof positive of man's evolutionary ancestry, can now safely be filed away under 'fiction.'"[13]

## Nebraska Man

In 1922, Harold Cook unearthed a single tooth in Nebraska. The tooth was dated at 1.7 to 5.5 million years old and classified as a fundamental link in the ape-to-human sequence. This theoretical specimen was nicknamed Nebraska Man. Indeed, the mind boggles, an ape-man from just one tooth! Parenthetically, this is a classic example of the amount of unbridled "interpretation" that goes on in this field of "science." A whole monkey-man was imagined from one tooth. Please, let that sink in. This is what happens. All the pent-up presuppositions and ambitions of the evolutionist are unleashed on the public because a tooth was found. Yes, it is incredible, but Darwinists get away with this kind of stuff all the time. Close parentheses. Oops . . . in 1928, Nebraska Man's tooth was determined to belong to an extinct pig.

## Peking Man

In 1927, near Peking (Beijing), China, Davidson Black dug up a single tooth and sometime later a partial skull. The find was touted as an ape-man transitional form which became known as Peking Man. He was all the rage among the true believers. Oops . . . French paleontologist Marcellin Boule, Director of the Museum of Natural History in Paris, determined that the much-ballyhooed missing link was in fact "nothing more than a battered monkey skull."[14] Engineer Ian Taylor writes, "One suspects that the only evolution that has occurred in the case of Peking Man has been in the imagination of those making the reconstruction."[15] As history has clearly shown, that's the only place macroevolution ever happens!

## Nutcracker Man

In 1959, Louis and Mary Leakey found a skull in East Africa ultimately nicknamed Nutcracker Man. It was publicized as yet another transitional link between ape and man. It was believed that Nutcracker Man was some 600,000 years old. He was initially dated at 1.75 million years old but subsequent testing dated him at 10,000 years. Parenthetically, here we have the dating game debacle illustrated. Often, bones and fossils are dated by the geological presuppositions of the strata in which they are found, and the strata are often dated by the evolutionary presuppositions of the bones and fossils found in them. Yes, you're correct; there is an obvious circularity there that seems to be lost on your average evolutionist. Close parentheses. Oops . . . Nutcracker Man is now seen by many as merely an extinct ape.

## Lucy

In 1974, anthropologist Donald Johanson found a tiny skeleton in northern Africa that he claimed was over three million years old and was the first ape to walk upright—yet another so-called missing link between primitive apes and mankind. The find was called *Lucy*. Oops . . . twenty years later, Johanson admitted . . .

> . . . that the knee joint cited as proof that Lucy walked upright was found more than two miles away and 200 feet lower in the strata! When further asked how he could be sure that the bones belonged to Lucy, he weakly replied, "Anatomical similarity."[16]

Blanchard notes . . .

> Lucy is a good example of the way in which articulate evolutionists have used popular media presentation to perfect the art of passing off guesswork as fact . . . [how] a stab in the dark has acquired the status of dogma.[17]

Johnson adds, "Instead of a fact we have speculative hypothesis . . . interpreted by persons strongly committed to proving evolution."[18] I have a compelling desire to paraphrase Ph.D. molecular biologist Douglas Axe once again: Trust science on the counting of moons and protons but where interpretation is required, better double-check the data.[19] This is a painfully obvious, non-negotiable axiom regarding all the historical sciences.

## Arguments from Imagination

As noted earlier, this is where we are with Darwinians. These guys believe evolution because they believe evolution. They have no intellectual category for non-evolution. Non-evolution is not a possibility. We are here, ergo evolution is true, and monkey-men must have existed because there is no other feasible way we could now be walking around on the planet. So, the data is always interpreted in light of that predetermined, unquestioned certainty.

Find a pig's tooth and it's extrapolated into an ape-man transitional form. Question, how is that possible? Answer, conclusions in search of anything that looks remotely like evidence. To question evolution is, as Ph.D. John Lennox writes, "tantamount to questioning what is, to them, sheer fact by virtue of philosophical necessity."[20] As we will see in the remainder of this chapter, evolutionists are not showing us any hard evidence; they're simply selling us a story dictated by their worldview. No hard facts are ever put forth, just the same old ideologically driven narrative. Yes, you're right, "Arguments from imagination are not evidence."[21]

Dig up some skeletal remains and several miles away a knee joint at a much lower depth, and what is the obvious conclusion? Well, it might as well be a missing link in the human evolutionary sequence. Why? Because we already know that evolution is true and, yeah, we need a link, really, really bad! Friend, this is not credible science by anyone's definition. This is pseudoscience! Macroevolution is pure ideology! It's "just another kind of fundamentalism."[22] True science follows the evidence wherever it leads. The facts are always the facts. The crucial issue is the interpretation of those facts. Evolutionary scientists have, as Lennox writes, "... wandered from doing science into myth-making—incoherent myths at that."[23]

Silvestru writes . . .

> It makes one wonder why the need for so much fraud if the evolution of humans is certain? The answer is obvious: fossils do not support the evolution of humans and apes from a common ancestor. It is the absence of evidence that forces frustrated anthropologists to explore every possible way to compensate for the lack of fossils . . . all the [nineteenth- and twentieth-century] data used . . . to support human evolution has since been rejected.[24]

I'm guessing you've never heard that fact before. Interesting, isn't it?

## Man, Monkey, and Banana

For those who rigorously shun evolutionary indoctrination and yeah, you know, just look around a bit, understand that man is not only outside the animal kingdom; he is in every conceivable way above it. There is no valid comparison in the unbiased mind. You may have heard it said that man and chimpanzees share 98-99% DNA. Just so you know, Ph.D. marine biologist Robert Carter writes that, "this is not true"[25] and continues . . .

> [T]here are entire gene families found in humans that are absent in chimps. This throws a monkey-wrench into evolutionary models for there have only been a few hundred thousand generations since we were supposedly the same species. [26]

This fact reveals that there is simply not enough "evolutionary time" available for natural selection to do its mystical-magical-Aesop-fable kind of thing between monkey and man. It is also claimed that man shares 50% DNA with, oh wait, bananas. What do these DNA sharing factoids really tell us? Not very much, I suspect. Maybe it simply reveals that a Genius Creator gets maximum variety out of His DNA code! The data points more to a common Designer than to a common ancestor. Again, the look-around test suffices for the thinking person. Without question, you and I are demonstrably unlike the chimp or his banana!

While Darwin and his minions have sought to bring man down, God has unmistakably set him up. This distinction between man and every other living thing on planet earth is not only observationally true, but is unequivocally asserted in the Genesis record. When God "formed man . . . and breathed into his nostrils the breath of life"[27] there is a sense of tenderness and intimacy absent in the rest of the creation account. And, of course, God declares that He "created man in His own image."[28] *The Message Bible* paraphrase helps make the point regarding the unique position of mankind: "God created human beings; He created them godlike, reflecting God's nature."[29] Job understood and gives voice to every self-aware and awakened soul, "The Spirit of God has made me, and the breath of the Almighty gives me life." [30] Regarding Genesis 2:18-24, Lennox writes, "It's interesting that the first lesson Adam was taught . . . is that he was fundamentally different from all other creatures."[31] Secular man must exert extraordinary intellectual energy to proactively "suppress"[32] that objective reality.

## The Look-Around Test

I sorely dislike stating the obvious but unfortunately this is sometimes necessary in countering the Jell-O like arguments of Darwinian evolution. Following is a concise list of attributes and abilities that set mankind wholly apart from the beasts. Clearly, this is not an exhaustive list but helps one to get some rudimentary sense of the gaping chasm existing between man and primate. I again condense and quote from John Blanchard's outstanding chapter on this matter in his book, *Does God Believe in Atheists?* Man . . .

> . . . walks uprightly, has vastly superior intelligence, is a historical and political being, is self-aware, thinks about meaning, purpose, and significance, uses propositional language, is capable of complex reasoning, has mathematical skills, has cultural and scientific achievements, has an aesthetic dimension, is endlessly creative, is not governed by instinct alone, is unique in his relationship with the opposite sex, [and] has a moral and spiritual dimension.[33]

Darwin's colleague and co-discoverer, Alfred Wallace, noted the inescapable distinction between man and the animal kingdom in writing "that man's higher capacities such as the human spirit, the mind, and the faculties of speech, art, music, mathematics, humor and morality were beyond the reach of natural selection."[34] Yeah, it's the look-around test. It obviously served Mr. Wallace quite well, as is true for most who take the time to practice it. Of course, his collaborator, Charles Darwin, refused to join him in that invaluable exercise.

## Fictions, Fables, Exaggerations, Scams, and Frauds

In the balance of the chapter, I want to briefly expose you to some of the other fictions, fables, tales, extrapolations, speculations, misrepresentations, exaggerations, erroneous inferences, scams, and frauds used to support the materialistic, macro-

Darwinian hypothesis. Yes, this is the best the Darwinists can do. Creationists would never be allowed to get away with such shoddy science. Wells writes, "When asked to list the evidence for Darwinian evolution, most people—including most biologists—give the same set of examples, because all of them learned biology from the same few textbooks."[35] All of these so-called evidences have appeared, and unbelievably, some still appear, in modern textbooks. Following are a few appalling examples summarized in part from Jonathan Wells' splendid book, *Icons of Evolution*, a must-read for anyone interested in truth as opposed to Darwinian duplicity.

## The Goo Guys

*First* . . . is the 1953 Miller-Urey experiment which purported to demonstrate the initial sequence of life's origin. Pretty heady stuff! The test sought to simulate Earth's primitive atmosphere and create the so-called building blocks of life by shooting an electric spark into the mix. This trial produced a few simple amino acids. Oops . . . for decades now, as Wells writes, ". . . most geochemists have been convinced that the experiment failed to simulate conditions on the early Earth, and thus has little or nothing to do with the origin of life."[36] Wells continues, "As Jon Cohen wrote in *Science* in 1995 many origin-of-life researchers now dismiss the 1953 experiment because 'the early atmosphere looked nothing like the Miller-Urey simulation.'"[37] In other words, all the experiment revealed was that Miller and Urey were remarkably adept at generating gunk in the bottom of their flasks.

Moreover, apart from the not-so-small detail of the simulated atmosphere being totally inaccurate in this experiment, it must be noted that amino acids are light years away from the staggering complexity of the information-rich DNA molecule and the nanotechnology of cellular life. Nobel Prize-winning molecular biologist Francis Crick, co-discoverer of the DNA molecule, gives us some small sense of just how complex the real building blocks of life truly are.

> Aware of modern life's nearly infinite complexity, Crick concluded that the earth was not old enough at 4.5 billion years to have had life gradually evolve completely on this planet . . . he preferred the "direct panspermia" concept.[38]

And this means that aliens seeded earth with complex life. Yeah, I know. But at least Crick understood that the separation between Miller-Urey's goo and complex life was nothing less than . . . yes, pun intended . . . galactic.

## Circular Reasoning

*Second* . . . is Darwin's assertion that macroevolution is the best explanation for the similarity of the limbs of animals (homology) with backbones (vertebrates) including appendages as varied as fins, wings, legs, and hands. This was a big deal to Darwin in establishing *proof* for evolution but ultimately this is no more than a subjective observation. Homology in no way proves evolution. Again, it's a barefaced example of a conclusion in search of evidence. Oops . . . yes, you're right, there is an obvious circularity to this line of reasoning, as Ph.D. Jonathan Sarfati writes . . .

> . . . evolutionists often define homologous as descended from a common ancestor. But this leads to circular reasoning if they then use homology as proof of common ancestors, since it becomes equivalent to: these features descended from a common ancestor, prove they descended from a common ancestor.[39]

Furthermore, there are insurmountable unresolved genetic, mechanistic, and developmental questions regarding the alleged common ancestry of radically diverse creatures—such as, yes, here's an interesting one, a cow and a whale. I know! But really, I'm not making it up. Google it for yourself!

## Proving Too Little

*Third* . . . We have Darwin's famed Galapagos finches. Although it is now widely acknowledged that these birds and their beaks had very little to do with Darwin's development of his evolutionary theories, they have achieved almost mythical status as a symbol for the efficacy of Darwin's hypothesis. Oops . . . the change of beak sizes among the finches has been shown to vacillate with changes in the climate exhibiting no long-term evolutionary transformation. And, yes, you're right, this is an example of microevolution (minor change within a species or population) not macroevolution (major change above the species level). No one denies that microevolution occurs. God endowed His creatures with tremendous genetic diversity in order to adapt to environmental changes. Darwin's renowned finches prove way too little except to point to the manifold genius of the Creator.

## Outright Fraud

*Fourth* . . . is the distasteful case of German biologist Ernest Haeckel's embryos. Darwin knew he had serious problems with the fossil record and no plausible mechanism to explain his theorized homologies from a common ancestor, but he considered Haeckel's work "by far the strongest single class of facts in favor of his theory."[40] Haeckel's drawings comparing embryos of various vertebrates revealed that they were effectively identical in their initial stages. Oops . . . it is now known that Darwin's favorite embryologist cherry-picked his samples and was less than discriminating in his drawings. Wells writes that eminent evolutionist "Stephen Jay Gould noted that Haeckel exaggerated the similarities by idealizations and omissions and concluded that his drawings are characterized by inaccuracies and outright falsification."[41] Embryologist Michael Richardson comments: "It looks like it's turning out to be one of the most famous fakes in biology."[42] Yikes, that said about what was, in Darwin's own words, the "strongest single class of facts in favor of his theory." It was fraud! No, the irony is not lost.

## Staging the Evidence

*Fifth* . . . is the classic textbook example of evolution at work—the peppered moth. In the 1950s, British biologist Bernard Kettlewell postulated that natural selection had changed the predominate color patterns of the peppered moth during the industrial revolution. This was due, he argued, to pollution-darkened tree trunks and the ease with which predatory birds could locate lighter colored moths resting on those trunks. This was vividly illustrated in most textbooks by various colored moths resting on light and dark tree trunks. Oops . . . in the wild, peppered moths do not rest on tree trunks. The photos were staged. While there could well be some truth to Kettlewell's assertions, evolutionary biologist Jerry Coyne notes "the fact that peppered moths do not rest on tree trunks alone invalidates Kettlewell's release-and-recapture experiments, as moths were released by placing them directly onto tree trunks."[43] Whatever conclusions are drawn from Kettlewell's work, it is clear that his experiment is dealing within the realm of microevolution, which, as we have repeatedly noted, no one denies occurs.

## So Many Erroneous Inferences, So Little Time

There is more that could be said about these and other so-called evidences for macro-Darwinian evolution, but I will leave it there. Considering all we've seen in this chapter regarding a variety of the highest profile data cited in favor of Darwin's hypothesis, some of Berlinski's words inescapably come to mind: "This is not a thesis calculated to set the blood racing."[44] Whereas, I might add, for every alive and awakened soul, David's shout of worship to his Creator-God in Psalm 29:9 is designed to do precisely that! "Everything says, 'Glory!'"

* * *

". . . there are thousands of scientists and intellectuals today who are convinced that in a fair science showdown, stripped bare of rhetoric and ideological noise . . . biblical creation outguns evolution."[45]

*David Catchpoole, Ph.D., Scientist, Lecturer, Author*

# Notes: Chapter 4

[1] Phillip E. Johnson, *Darwin on Trial* (Downers Grove, IL: Intervarsity Press, 2010), 163.
[2] David Berlinski, *The Devil's Delusion* (New York, NY: Basic Books, 2008), 156.
[3] Emil Silvestru, "The Fossil Record," in *Evolutions Achilles Heels* (Powder Springs, GA: Creation Books, 2014), 144.
[4] Jonathan Wells, *Icons of Evolution* (Washington D.C.: Regnery Publishing, 2002), 225.
[5] Richard Dawkins, *The God Delusion* (Boston, MA: Houghton Mifflin, 2006), 5.
[6] Ibid.
[7] Richard Dawkins, *The Blind Watchmaker* (New York, NY: W. W. Norton & Company, 1986), 6.
[8] Dawkins, *The God Delusion*, 5.
[9] John 8:12.
[10] John Blanchard, *Does God Believe in Atheists*? (Darlington, UK: Evangelical Press, 2000), 78-110.
[11] Marvin Lubenow, *Bones of Contention* (Cranleigh, UK: Baker Books), 65.
[12] Lee Strobel, *The Case For a Creator* (Grand Rapids, MI: Zondervan, 2004), 61.
[13] Blanchard, 103.
[14] Ibid, 104.
[15] Ian Taylor, *In the Minds of Men* (Zimmerman, MN:TFE Publishing,1984), 237.
[16] Blanchard, 106.
[17] Ibid.
[18] Phillip E. Johnson, privately circulated article cited by Bowden, *Science vs Evolution*, 227.
[19] Douglas Axe, *Undeniable* (New York, NY: Harper One, 2016), 38.
[20] John Lennox, *God's Undertaker* (Oxford, England: Lion Books, 2009), 99.
[21] Sean McDowell, *Understanding Intelligent Design* (Eugene, OR: Harvest House, 2008), 27.
[22] Johnson, *Darwin On Trial*, 33.
[23] Lennox, *God's Undertaker*, 43.
[24] Silvestru, 148.
[25] Robert Carter, "Genetics and DNA," in *Evolutions Achilles Heels*, 74.
[26] Ibid.
[27] Genesis 2:7.
[28] Genesis 1:27.
[29] Eugene Peterson, *The Message Bible* (Colorado Springs; NavPress: 2002), Genesis 1:27.
[30] Job 33:4.
[31] John Lennox, *Seven Days That Divide The World* (Grand Rapids, MI: Zondervan, 2016), 71.
[32] Romans 1:18.

[33] Blanchard, 324-330.
[34] Jonathan Sarfati, *The Greatest Hoax on Earth* (Atlanta, GA: Creation Book Publishers, 2010), 150.
[35] Wells, 6.
[36] Ibid., 11.
[37] Ibid., 21.
[38] Cited in Jeremy L. Walter, "Mechanical Engineering," in *In Six Days: Why Fifty Scientists Choose to Believe in Creation*, (Green Forest, AR: Master Books, 2001), 18.
[39] Sarfati, 90-91.
[40] Cited in Wells, 82.
[41] Ibid., 94.
[42] Elizabeth Pennisi, *Haeckel's Embryos; Fraud Rediscovered.* Science, vol. 277, 1997, 1435.
[43] Cited in Wells, 153.
[44] Berlinski, 53.
[45] Cited in Sarfati, 10.

# ~five~

## Fearfully & Wonderfully Coded

"I think the information revolution taking place in biology is sounding the death knell for Darwinism and chemical evolutionary theories. The attempt to explain the origin of life solely from chemical constituents is effectively dead now. . . . Information transcends matter and energy. . . . Information is the hallmark of mind."[1]

*Stephen C. Meyer, Ph.D. Philosophy of Science*

"The result of these cumulative efforts to investigate the cell—to investigate life at the molecular level—is a loud, clear, piercing cry of 'design!' The result is so unambiguous and so significant that it must be ranked as one of the greatest achievements in the history of science."[2]

*Michael J. Behe, Ph.D. Biology, Professor of Biochemistry*

". . . we have only to see a few letters of the alphabet spelling our name in the sand to recognize at once the work of an intelligent agent. How much more likely, then, is the existence of an intelligent Creator behind human DNA, the colossal biological database that contains no fewer than 3.5 billion 'letters'—the longest 'word' yet discovered?"[3]

*John C. Lennox, Ph.D. Mathematics, Philosophy*

"Information theory is a whole new branch of science that has effectively destroyed the last underpinnings of evolution. . . ."[4]

*Jonathan D. Sarfati, Ph.D. Physical Chemistry*

If I were smarter, I would definitely have a better subtitle. I recently read Thomas Nagel's book entitled *Mind & Cosmos.* Nagel is a well regarded contemporary philosopher, and has without question crafted the best subtitle I've ever seen. It reads, *Why the Materialist Neo-Darwinian Conception of Nature is Almost Certainly False.* This, mind you, from an avowed atheist.

While Nagel runs at the macroevolutionary question from a radically different perspective than I, we both arrive at the same place. He says the hypothesis ". . . cannot provide the basic form of intelligibility for this world."[5] Yeah, he says it so much better than I would. I just say it's laughable. No matter how one says it, reductionism, shorthand for Darwinian materialism, is wholly inadequate in explaining human life, and again, quoting Nagel, is a "worldview . . . ripe for displacement."[6] That's what I've been saying through the first four chapters of this book, albeit not quite as well as he.

## A Signature in the Cell

Another terrific subtitle I encountered of late is Anthony Flew's for his book entitled *There Is A God.* The subtitle reads, *How the World's Most Notorious Atheist Changed His Mind.* Flew repudiated his atheism due in large part to the staggering complexity of human DNA. He is quoted as saying he merely followed the evidence where it led. Yes, of course, it's what rational people do. Regarding his new-found theism, Flew writes, ". . . this is the world picture, as I see it, that has emerged from modern science."[7] He is quoted as saying that "a super-intelligence is the only good explanation of the origin of life and complexity of nature."[8] I feel an urgent need to revisit, yet again, Ph.D. Stephen

Meyer's words, "Science done right points to God."[9] Yes, yes, yes, and amen!

Without question, God's fingerprints are everywhere evident in the created order. But the ongoing discovery of His absolutely astonishing handiwork at the cellular and molecular levels is beginning to turn faultfinding atheists into admiring theists. It's the title of Meyer's remarkable book, *Signature in the Cell*. The dizzying sophistication of the internal workings of the single cell is unavoidably and unmistakably shouting for all creation to clearly hear and understand—*Made by Yahweh!* The genius resident within the cell is indeed God's biological autograph.

## Exquisite Nanotechnology

In 1953, English scientists James Watson and Francis Crick elucidated the structure of DNA and won a Nobel Prize. Biology has never really been the same. The DNA molecule contains all the information necessary to build you. There are six feet of DNA coiled inside every one of your body's 40-100 trillion cells (except red blood cells). The coded algorithms stored in the DNA of each cell carry so much information that it would take 1,000 books each 1,000 pages in length to record it. Ph.D. Francis Collins writes that the live reading of the information in the DNA of one human cell would take "at a rate of three letters per second . . . 31 years, reading day and night."[10] And all 3.5 billion characters, 7 billion bits of information, would easily fit inside something much smaller than the period at the end of this sentence.

As compared to our most advanced computers, Meyer writes, ". . . the digital information in DNA [is] only part of a complex information-processing system . . . that mirrors and exceeds our own in its complexity, storage density, and logic of design."[11] This is, as Ph.D. Paul Davies rightly comments, "exquisite nanotechnology."[12] We intuitively grasp that information and nanotechnology could never be the result of natural selection acting upon undirected random mutation. It can only be the result of Genius!

There is, as biology Ph.D. Robert Carter says, a "hyper-complexity" to the DNA molecule. He writes . . .

> When we sequenced the human genome, we thought we would then understand how the genome works. This was a naïve error. What we had done was sequence the linear strings of nucleotides only. This was only the first dimension of a genome that operates in at least four dimensions.[13]

I won't attempt to develop the dimensional intricacies of DNA because I can't. But if you're able to worship on a much higher intellectual plain than I, please follow the endnote.

## A Self-Evident Truth

Many have said it: Darwinism needs life to be simple. It's not. Regarding the human genome, Carter says, ". . . this system is one of the wonders of the universe."[14] So, here's a question for your average man on the street, or even your average seven-year-old on the playground: Do coded algorithms and interdependent, four-dimensional operating systems arise spontaneously by any known natural process? This is not a hard question. In fact, it's a layup. And yet its instinctively obvious answer seems to escape many. It's a clear refusal to join Flew's lead in simply following the evidence where it leads. Regrettably, this is not uncommon among Darwinian biologists.

Bill Gates, famous founder of Microsoft, says, "DNA is like a computer program but far, far more advanced than any software ever created."[15] So, from where does code arise? Ask even the humblest software writer and that individual will not hesitate to let you know—code comes from a highly developed intellect. Which comes first: mind or code? The answer, of course, again is self-evident. Origin-of-life researcher Bernd-Olaf Kuppers could not have said it better: "The problem of the origin of life is clearly basically equivalent to the problem of the origin of biological information."[16] Meyer adds, "If you can't explain where the information comes from, you haven't explained life, because it's the information that makes molecules into something that actually functions."[17] Scientists who've looked at the data through a Darwinian lens "justifiably expected randomness and simplicity, but discovered depths of elegance, order, and complexity."[18] This is an insurmountable problem for Darwin's hypothesis.

## Authentic Wonderment

As noted, it was once assumed that life at the cellular level was extraordinarily simple. The cell was a *"black box"* to scientists, meaning no one had a clue what was going on inside. Historically, biologists have, in the main, assumed that life's origin was essentially chemical in nature. A few fortuitous, yet basically simple, chemical interactions might have given rise to the building blocks of life in a mythical primordial soup. Cells were viewed as "homogeneous and structure-less globules of protoplasm, amorphous sacs of chemical jelly."[19] Well, that was an erroneous assumption of cosmic proportions. The black box has now been opened, and molecular biologists are filled with authentic wonderment at the genius-level engineering they've discovered within. Author Sean McDowell is right: "The level of engineering inside the cell so far exceeds our own expertise that we are like cavemen looking at a space shuttle."[20]

Regarding the brilliance discovered within the cell, a language of design has become commonplace among molecular biologists . . .

> taking expressions . . . from communication theory, electrical engineering, and computer science. The vocabulary of modern molecular and cell biology includes . . . terms [like] "genetic code," "genetic information," "transcription," "translation," "editing enzymes," "signal-transduction circuitry," "feedback loops," and "information processing system."[21]

Even militant atheist Richard Dawkins acknowledges that "Apart from differences in jargon, the pages of a molecular-biology journal might be interchanged with those of a computer-engineering journal."[22]

## The Unavoidable Inference

So, humanity finally builds a microscope sophisticated enough to pierce the "black box" of the molecular world and what is the most transparently obvious discovery? An Engineer of unparalleled intellect! Lennox is right at this point: ". . . science—far from making God redundant and irrelevant as atheists often affirm—actually confirms his existence. . . ."[23] It is evident to the thinking person that before space, time, matter, energy, physics, and chemistry, there was Mind. Biological information, language, and design form a category infinitely above and distinct from lifeless matter, chemicals, and energy. True science always looks for the inference to the best explanation. The clear inference is this: there must be a genius Engineer before there could ever be ingenious engineering. This is not rocket science. Children can, and do, understand such intuitive realities.

As noted, molecular biology naturally evokes the parlance of design. It's where the mind unavoidably goes in studying the cell. Behe writes . . .

> . . . life is based on machines—machines made of molecules! In short, highly sophisticated molecular machines control every cellular process. Thus, the details of life are finely calibrated, and the machinery of life enormously complex.[24]

Then he tells us how Darwinists account for all the information and intricate design within the cell—oh, that's right, they can't! Behe continues . . .

> . . . if you search the scientific literature on evolution, and you focus your search on the question of how molecular machines—the basis of life—developed, you find an eerie and complete silence. The complexity of life's foundation has paralyzed science's attempt to account for it; molecular machines raise an as-yet-impenetrable barrier to Darwinism's universal reach.[25]

He concludes, ". . . for Darwinian theory of evolution to be true, it has to account for the molecular structure of life . . . it does not."[26]

## Darwin's Leg Up

As you probably know, Darwin never attempted to explain the origin of life—that very first living thing which has allegedly given rise to every other living thing. You must appreciate the fact that Darwin's theory simply assumes life. Darwinian theory does not touch on the origin of life. It just presupposes it. It's my sense that this is not widely understood. It is, by the way, a most convenient development for the materialists. To simply start talking about macroevolution without having to offer a coherent commentary on life's origin with its copious amounts of biological information and inherent irreducible complexity at the molecular level. That's quite a leg up—sort of a free ride around the patently inexplicable! Allow me to give you five quotes to help underscore and quantify where modern science is on this question of the origin of life:

- Ph.D. John Lennox writes: "Darwinian evolution presupposes the existence of a mutating replicator in order to get things going in the first place. Hence Darwinian evolution, by definition, cannot be an explanation for the existence of the very thing without which it itself cannot get started. . . . In fact, a plausible theory of the origin of life does not exist."[27]

- Origin of life expert Professor Walter Bradley says that "... the mind-boggling difficulties in bridging the yawning gap between non-life and life mean that there may very well be no potential of ever finding a theory for how life could have arisen spontaneously ... absolutely overwhelming evidence points toward an intelligence behind life's creation."[28]
- Ph.D. Michael Behe writes, "... Darwin's idea of a 'tree of life'—where a single primordial cell gave rise to all subsequent organisms—is dead. The DNA sequence data cannot be made to fit with that idea."[29]
- Science journalist John Horgan has stated that "scientists have no idea how inanimate matter on our little planet coalesced into living creatures.... Science you might say has discovered that our existence is infinitely improbable and hence a miracle."[30]
- Nobel Prize winner Francis Crick who, as noted earlier, discovered the molecular structure of DNA writes, "An honest man, armed with all the knowledge available to us now, could only state that in some sense, the origin of life appears at the moment to be almost a miracle, so many are the conditions which would have had to have been satisfied to get it going."[31]

## More Darwinian Folklore

Crick wrote the above sentence in 1981. Well, first, that's ancient history when it comes to molecular science, and secondly, the case for the theory of a naturalistic origin of life has only gotten dramatically worse. Also note that Horgan and Crick both were compelled to invoke the word *miracle*. It looked like a miracle in 1981 and looks even more like a miracle almost forty years on.

As you probably know, Darwin casually postulated a theoretical "warm little pond"[32] where, against all reasonable odds, life could have serendipitously "emerged" from non-life. Professor Phillip Johnson points out the obvious here in that "... chemicals do not produce offspring."[33] The pre-biotic soup, he continues, "... is an element of scientific folklore"[34] for which there is not a shred of empirical evidence. And regarding random chance as a credible hypothesis for the emergence of life from non-life, Meyer says, "Virtually all origin-of-life experts have utterly rejected that approach."[35] He continues by stating that while it's true that "scenario is still alive among people who don't know the facts ... there's no merit to it. ... There's a minimal complexity threshold."[36]

## Dead on Arrival

Darwin himself commented on a "complexity threshold." He wrote, "If it could be demonstrated that any complex organ existed which could not possibly have been formed by numerous, successive, slight modification, my theory would absolutely break down."[37] Little did Darwin know his theory was dead on arrival relative to that first simple cell, the theorized ancestor of all life on the planet. For, as modern science has discovered, there are no simple cells. Every last so-called simple cell is strikingly complex. Darwin's theory dies right here. It's just all over at this point. Evolutionary theory cannot cope with the biological information and irreducible complexity of molecular life.

## The Numbers Don't Lie

And let's talk about the math for just a moment. There's a reason Darwinists hate it when you bring up the numbers regarding their assertion that randomness can get you from chemicals to an alive molecule. The probabilities of lifeless chemicals giving rise to a living organism are simply outrageously absurd. They are outside the realm of reason. They are a statistical impossibility, not to mention a logical impossibility. The odds of life from non-life expand beyond any sort of meaningful comprehension—requiring, as Ph.D. Thomas Nagel writes, "probabilistic contortions."[38] Meyer adds ...

> the probabilities of forming a rather short functional protein at random would be one chance in a hundred thousand trillion trillion trillion trillion trillion trillion trillion trillion trillion trillion trillion. That's a 10 with 125 zeroes after it! And that would be only one protein molecule—a minimally complex cell would need between three hundred and five hundred protein molecules.... To suggest chance against those odds is really to invoke a naturalistic miracle.[39]

Yeah, there's that word again—miracle. Please indulge me a bit more on the arithmetic. All of us really do need to get a sense of just how impossible life from non-life is. We should clearly understand that materialism, naturalism, and macroevolutionary theory cannot begin to rationally account for the biological information and complexity required for life at the molecular level. We need to feel the weight of the colossal improbabilities involved here. So, at the risk of losing some readers, let's jump in. Trust me, it will be worth it. You will have a much better grasp of just how utterly preposterous it is to postulate life from non-life by chance alone. In having some conceptual feel for the probabilities involved, you can no longer be fooled by scientific bluster and speculative mumbo jumbo. The numbers are the numbers. They don't lie.

## One Chance in $10^{40,861}$

Some years ago, Ph.D. mathematician William Dembski "calculated the maximum number of events that could have actually taken place during the history of the observable universe. He did this to establish an upper boundary of the probabilistic resources that might be available to produce an event by chance." [40]

Based on Dembski's calculations at that time, there were . . .

- $10^{80}$ elementary particles in the observable universe;
- $10^{17}$ number of seconds since the theorized big bang;
- $10^{43}$ number of possible interactions per second in the universe.[41]

By taking these three factors into account, Dembski arrives at the "total number of events that could have taken place in the observable universe since the origin of the universe at $10^{140}$. This then provided a measure of the probabilistic resources of the entire observable universe."[42] Meyer summarizes: "The probability of producing the proteins necessary to build a minimally complex cell—or the genetic information necessary to produce those proteins . . . at best, 1 chance in $10^{40,861}$."[43] This number is so large as to be beyond meaning and comprehension. It defies physical representation. We don't have to be mathematicians to see the stupefying disparity between $10^{140}$ and $10^{40,861}$.

The upshot is, this ain't ever happened and it ain't ever going to happen! To assert otherwise is nonsense of the highest order—a desperate appeal to brute luck, or more accurately, blind faith. It's why scientists keep invoking that word, *miracle*. Meyer concludes . . .

> The complexity of the events that origin-of-life researchers need to explain exceeds the probabilistic resources of the entire universe. In other words, the universe itself does not possess the probabilistic resources necessary to render probable the origin of biological information by chance alone.[44]

Bam! These hard-number realities simply destroy the Darwinian paradigm. As Ph.D. philosopher Alvin Plantinga says, "Things don't look hopeful for the Darwinian naturalists."[45]

## It's Just Over

The hard math gives credence to Ph.D. mathematician and astrophysicist Fred Hoyle's famous quip that "the spontaneous emergence of life on earth . . . is about as likely as a tornado sweeping through a junkyard and assembling a Boeing 747 out of the debris."[46] I might add, not merely an assembled 747, but a functioning one!

I do apologize for getting up into the weeds with the numbers, but this is just a knock-down argument against naturalism, materialism, scientism, and macro-Darwinian theory. It's just over. There's nowhere to run and nowhere to hide. No reasonable person argues against such odds. Is anything less probable in the entire known cosmos than life spontaneously emerging from non-life? No. So where does that leave one? I would submit either in prostrate worship of the One who has a reputation for doing miracles (you know, that word that keeps coming up) or in abject denial of the obvious on par with the man sprinting over the precipice disavowing the law of gravity.

## God or Magic

Back to the DNA molecule for a moment to further highlight the improbabilities of the self-assemblage of molecular life. Here, we have an intractable Catch-22 impasse. McDowell quantifies it perfectly and please take a moment to seriously ponder his questions. He writes . . .

> DNA depends on protein for proper functioning, yet protein relies upon DNA for correct sequencing. Protein cannot arise apart from DNA, yet DNA needs protein to function. So, which came first? How did two separate systems arise simultaneously that rely on one another for survival and function?[47]

There is no plausible materialistic, naturalistic, macroevolutionary answer to these questions. Moreover, the energy needed for these molecular processes is supplied by the ATP synthase motor, which, by the way, cannot be produced without instructions in the DNA. Appealing to chance for the simultaneous emergence of DNA-dependent protein and protein-dependent DNA fueled by DNA-dependent ATP synthase motors exacerbates the odds which, as noted earlier, already exhaust the probabilistic resources of the known universe. If all three are not present and functioning in concert, there is no life. Yes, you're right, we're right back to miracle again. It's irrefutable—molecular biology demands a Genius Engineer or a magic wand!

## Devolution

While we're in the genetics neighborhood, I'd like to conclude the chapter by mentioning a couple of related subjects. First, is Michael Behe's research published in his must-read book entitled *The Edge of Evolution*. The question Behe was seeking to answer is "What, exactly, can evolution do?" Not much as it turns out. Behe writes, "The power of natural selection coupled with random variation has been grossly oversold to the modern public. . . . There are radical limits on the efficacy of random mutation."[48] He reports on studies of E. coli . . .

> subject of the most extensive laboratory evolution study ever conducted. Duplicating about seven times a day . . . having been grown continuously in flasks for over thirty thousand generations . . . equivalent to about a million human-years. And what has evolution wrought? Mostly devolution . . . it's easier for evolution to break things than make things.[49]

It's an indisputable fact. Most mutations are harmful and the few that are beneficial break genes. Ph.D. biochemist John Kramer writes, ". . . mutations observed on a molecular level such as DNA, are predominately disruptive, and always with a loss of, not gain in, information and complexity."[50] If you examine evolutionary examples that are commonly cited, such as antibiotic resistance or the adaptation of saltwater stickleback fish to freshwater, for instance, you will find that what is being touted as evolution is, in fact, devolution—the genome is going backwards, not forwards. Ph.D. physiologist Donald Batten writes, ". . . we are being given 'broken' organisms as examples of adaptive mutations and natural selection."[51]

## Why Aren't We Dead 100 Times Over?

Which is the perfect sequitur to my second related subject—genetic meltdown. Macroevolutionary dogma demands that, as Batten writes . . .

> the mutation rate in organisms be quite low, on the order of one per individual per generation or less. Recognizing that most mutations were deleterious, they [evolutionists] had to assume that there were not many of them. . . . However, in recent years the mutation rate has been measured and it is at least 50-fold higher than assumed by evolutionary ideology. [52]

The high rate of detrimental mutations, Ph.D. geneticist John Sanford states, "is relentless and is destroying us, not creating us. We are headed for extinction, along with every other complex organism."[53] Batten concludes: "A process that steadily degrades a genome cannot produce a better organism in the long run. Sanford's analysis is devastating to the evolutionary paradigm."[54]

I want to make sure we understand. We're not evolving. We're devolving. We are, quite literally, moving toward extinction one genetic mutation at a time. When he juxtaposed assumed long eons of evolutionary time to real-world human genome mutation rates, Ph.D. geneticist Alexey Kondrashov asked, "Why aren't we dead 100 times over?"[55] The answer to his question is that, contrary to the long ages of time required by the theory of evolution, "the human genome hasn't been around long enough to deteriorate to lethal levels . . . [it] would already be fatally compromised if it had been around for many thousands of generations."[56] Carter estimates that humanity has been around about a "6000-year/200 generation time frame."[57] Sound familiar?

## Can't Get from Monkey to Man

Thirdly, and very briefly, science has discovered a genetic mutational speed limit, so to speak. It's called Haldane's dilemma and has never been satisfactorily resolved. In the 1950s J.B.S. Haldane found that, "beneficial evolution is too slow to explain large-scale biological transformation in the available time, even given the claimed evolutionary timescale."[58] In short, Haldane's work reveals that it is impossible to get from chimp to man even with the speculated deep time of evolutionary theory. Moreover, with the relatively recent sequencing of the human Y chromosome, researchers have noted that there is, as Safarti writes, "unexpected 'extraordinary divergence' from the chimp Y chromosome. . . ."[59] This is yet another insoluble genetic problem for the "microbes to the microbiologist" hypothesis.

## Mythical Stories Vs. Genetic Realities

Fourthly, you may have heard the commonly told account of mankind suffering a near extinction event within the not-too-distant, theorized evolutionary past. According to this folklore (the data does not support the hypothesis), only about 10,000 survivors of Homo erectus came out of Africa and rapidly evolved into modern man. Why this mythical story? Evolutionists are, as Carter writes, "trying to explain the lack of diversity among people spread across the world."[60] For, as he adds, human genetics reveal that we were not millions of years in the making, but "that we came from a small population in the recent past."[61]

Wait, I've read about a "small population in the recent past" somewhere. Where was that? Oh yes, I remember—it was in the

Genesis account of creation! I know this is a shock to many, but human genetics actually "supports the biblical account quite well,"[62] writes Carter. He concludes . . .

> There is abundant evidence in the genes of modern man for the creation of two original people (Adam and Eve), a population bottleneck a few thousand years later (during Noah's flood), and a subdivision of the population a few generations after that (at Babel), with the subsequent single dispersal of humanity across the globe. Not only that, but the rate of mutation, the distribution of mutations, and the fragility of the ultra-complex computer operating system called the human genome all testify to the youth of that system.[63]

## The New Explanation is the Old Explanation

In closing this chapter, Batten sums up well, "The more we learn about . . . complex genetics and biochemistry . . . the harder it becomes to believe the evolutionary notion."[64] Behe adds, "Darwin looks more and more forlorn. . . . The intransigence of the problem cannot be alleviated; it will only get worse. . . . The need for a new kind of explanation grows more apparent."[65] The new explanation is, of course, the old explanation. We've had it all along. God gave it to us through the pen of Moses. Regarding the irreducibly, interwoven complexity, and ingenious design of the single cell, Meyer says it perfectly: "Only theism can provide an intellectually satisfying causal explanation. . . ."[66]

King David didn't have a microscope. He didn't know about God's engineering genius at the cellular level. He really had no idea just how "fearfully and wonderfully made"[67] he was, but he knew well what is "evident within"[68] every man, from his DNA on up. Yes, that's right, "Everything says, 'Glory!'"

* * *

"We're deliciously complex at the molecular level. . . . We don't understand ourselves. . . . There is still a metaphysical, magical element. . . . What really astounds me is the architecture of life . . . the system is extremely complex. It's like it was designed. . . . There's a huge intelligence there. I don't see that as being unscientific."[69]

*Eugene Myers, Ph.D., Computer Science and Bioinformatician*

# Notes: Chapter 5

[1] Cited in Lee Strobel, *The Case For a Creator* (Grand Rapids, MI: Zondervan, 2004), 243-244.
[2] Michael Behe, *Darwin's Black Box*, (New York, NY: Touchstone, 1996), 232-233.
[3] John Lennox, *God and Stephen Hawking* (Oxford, England: Lion Hudson, 2014), 75.
[4] Jonathan Sarfati, *The Greatest Hoax on Earth* (Atlanta, GA: Creation Book Publishers, 2010), 44.
[5] Thomas Nagel, *Mind & Cosmos* (New York, NY: Oxford University Press, 2012), Book Jacket.
[6] Nagel, 12.
[7] Anthony Flew, *There Is A God* (New York, NY: Harper Collins Publishers, 2008), 88.
[8] Cited in John Lennox, *God's Undertaker* (Oxford, England: Lion Books, 2009), 10.
[9] Cited in Strobel, 77.
[10] Francis Collins, *The Language of God* (New York, NY: Free Press, 2006), 1.
[11] Steven Meyer, *Signature in the Cell* (New York, NY: Harper Collins Publishers, 2010), 14.
[12] Paul Davies, *The Goldilocks Enigma* (Great Britain: The Penguin Press, 20116), 192.
[13] Robert Carter, "Genetics and DNA," in *Evolutions Achilles Heels* (Powder Springs, GA: Creation Books, 2014) 60.
[14] Ibid., 65.
[15] Bill Gates, *The Road Ahead* (New York, NY: Viking Press, 1995), 188.
[16] Bernd-Olaf Kuppers, *Information & the Origin of Life* (Cambridge, MA: MIT Press, 1990), 170-172.
[17] Cited in Strobel, 225.
[18] Michael Behe, *The Edge of Evolution* (New York, NY; Free Press, 2008), 190.
[19] Ernst Haeckel, cited in Meyer, *Signature in the Cell*, 44.
[20] Sean McDowell, *Understanding Intelligent Design* (Eugene, OR: Harvest House, 2008), 134.
[21] Meyer, 21.
[22] Richard Dawkins, *River Out of Eden* (New York, NY: Basic Books, 1995), 17.
[23] John Lennox, *Seven Days That Divide The World* (Grand Rapids, MI: Zondervan, 2016), 13.
[24] Behe, *Darwin's Black Box*, 4-5.
[25] Ibid., 5.
[26] Ibid., 25.
[27] Lennox, *Seven Days That Divided the World*, 173.
[28] Cited in Strobel, 41.
[29] Michael Behe, Foreword of *Darwin on Trial* (Downers Grove, IL: Intervarsity Press, 1991, 17.
[30] John Horgan, "A Holiday Made for Believing," *New York Times* (December 25, 2002).
[31] Francis Crick, *Life Itself* (New York, NY: Simon and Schuster, 1981), 88.
[32] Cited in Phillip E. Johnson, *Darwin on Trial* (Downers Grove, IL: Intervarsity Press, 2010), 130.

[33] Ibid., 131.
[34] Ibid.
[35] Cited in Strobel, 229.
[36] Ibid.
[37] Charles Darwin, *On the Origin of Species*, (New York, NY: New York University Press, 6th ed. 1988), 154.
[38] Nagel, 128.
[39] Cited in Strobel, 229.
[40] Meyer, 213-217.
[41] William Dembski, *The Design Inference* as cited by Stephen Meyer, *Signature in the Cell*, 216.
[42] Meyer, 216-217.
[43] Ibid., 213, 219.
[44] Ibid., 219.
[45] Cited in Strobel, 269.
[46] Cited in David Berlinski, *The Devil's Delusion* (New York, NY: Basic Books, 2008), 140-141.
[47] McDowell, 129.
[48] Behe, *The Edge of Evolution*, 3,4,13.
[49] Ibid., 15-16.
[50] John K. G. Kramer, "Biochemistry," in *In Six Days: Why Fifty Scientists Choose to Believe in Creation*, (Green Forest, AR: Master Books, 2001) 47.
[51] Donald Batten, "Natural Selection," in *Evolutions Achilles Heels*, 40.
[52] Ibid., 39.
[53] Cited in Batten, Donald. 39.
[54] Ibid., 40.
[55] Cited in Sarfati, 57.
[56] Ibid., 58.
[57] Carter, Robert. 68.
[58] Sarfati, 56.
[59] Ibid., 55.
[60] Carter, Robert. 67.
[61] Ibid.
[62] Ibid., 77.
[63] Ibid.
[64] Batten, Donald. 28.
[65] Behe, *Darwin's Black Box*, 73.
[66] Cited in Strobel, 74.
[67] Psalm 139:14.
[68] Romans 1:19.
[69] Lennox, *God's Undertaker*, 176.

# ~six~

## Smart People Talking a Bit More

This is a different sort of chapter. It's some stuff I couldn't stuff into the previous chapters but felt I would be doing you an enormous disservice if I didn't share more of what these knowledgeable people have to say. What follows is a collection of interesting and pertinent insights loosely organized under several category headings.

Prepare to astonish your friends and colleagues with pithy quotes and thought-provoking (often worship-provoking) commentary. These are really, really, bright people who know what they're talking about. Admittedly, I don't know anything about Larry Eubank, a random guy from Indiana I'm quoting, but he sounds rather clever to me.

# Materialism, Naturalism, Scientism, Macro-Darwinian Ideology

"All [of] Darwin's evidence ... was, in the last analysis, purely circumstantial."[1]
*Michael Denton, Ph.D. Biologist*

"Darwin['s] ... theory can't possibly be defended as clearly and convincingly as it can be refuted."[2]
*Douglas Axe, Ph.D. Molecular Biologist*

"... discontent with traditional Darwinism rumbles among many scientists who think most intently about evolutionary issues."[3]
*Michael J. Behe, Ph.D. Biology, Professor of Biochemistry*

Regarding the scientific establishment—"... [they] are devoted to protecting Darwinism rather than testing it. ... [I]t is the official creation story of modern culture. The scientific priesthood that has authority to interpret the official creation story gains immense cultural influence thereby. ... The experts therefore have a vested interest in protecting the story ..."[4]
*Phillip E. Johnson, Author and Professor of Law, University of California*

"As things stand, at the present time, we are in urgent need of the de-mythologization of science." [5]
*John Durant, Ph.D. Historian, Philosopher*

"... evolution is not adhered to on scientific grounds at all. Rather, it is clung to, though flying in the face of reason, with an incredible, fanatical, and irrational religious fervor."[6]
*Ker Thomson, Sc.D. Geophysics*

"Many . . . biologists believe in Darwinian evolution because that's what they learned from their textbooks. These biologists suffer from the 'specialist effect'—They realize that Darwinian evolution cannot adequately explain what they know in their own field but assume that it explains what they don't know in others."[7]
*Jonathan Wells, Ph.D. Religious Studies, Molecular Biology*

Regarding Darwinian bias—"It is surely a curious inversion of the normal scientific process to assume the truth of what you want to prove and on that basis discredit evidence that is brought against it."[8]
*John C. Lennox, Ph.D. Mathematics, Philosophy*

Regarding Darwinian bias—"Pseudoscientists . . . find what they expect to find."[9]
*Phillip E. Johnson, Author and Professor of Law, University of California*

Regarding Darwinian bias—". . . once a community has elevated a theory into a self-evident truth, its defense becomes irrelevant and there is no longer any point in having to establish its validity by reference to empirical facts."[10]
*Michael Denton, Ph.D. Biologist*

"The evolutionary 'big picture' is . . . a self-reinforcing paradigm, in which most scientists and intellectuals believe it, essentially because most scientists and intellectuals believe it."[11]
*Jonathan D. Sarfati, Ph.D. Physical Chemistry*

"What is being passed off as 'science' turns out to be nothing more than a faith-based worldview that is hostile to the truth of Scripture."[12]
*John MacArthur, Theologian, Pastor, Author*

"Evolution is usually referred to as a theory, but in strictly scientific terms this is . . . going too far, because as Collin Patterson [Senior Paleontologist at the British Museum of Natural History] makes clear, it is not possible to prove or refute what it teaches."[13]
*John Blanchard, Christian Theologian, Apologist, Author*

"[Darwinism] . . . like some primordial jelly . . . is both squishy and constantly in motion. Terms, claims, and stories multiply unceasingly."[14]
*David Berlinski, Ph.D. Philosopher, Mathematician*

"Scientists who utterly reject evolution may be one of our fastest growing controversial minorities. . . . Many of the scientists supporting this position hold impressive credentials in science."[15]
*Larry Hatfield writing in* Science Digest

". . . biblical theism . . . far from involving intellectual suicide, makes more sense of the data than does atheistic reductionism."[16]
*John C. Lennox, Ph.D. Mathematics, Philosophy*

"I am always taken aback by the unquestioning certainty displayed by evolutionists in the face of a theory so fundamentally, intuitively preposterous; by the solemn assurances of TV broadcasts on nature that their fairy-tale rationalizations are 'science'; and by the intellectual thuggery of college professors who insist that evolution is scientific fact and that we must believe it. . . ."[17]
*Larry Eubank, random guy from Jeffersonville, Indiana, USA*

"It takes a greater degree of blind faith to believe in evolution than in the creation model of the Bible."[18]
*Ariel Roth, Ph.D. Biologist*

"... evolution survives as a paradigm only as long as the evidence is picked and chosen and the great pool of data that is accumulating on life is ignored. As the depth and breadth of human knowledge increases it ... [is] pointing to the conclusion that life is the result of design."[19]
*Timothy Standish, Ph.D. Biologist*

"Like Freud and Marx, Darwin has suffered from becoming a belief system. . . ."[20]
*A.S. Byatt, Award-winning English author*

"In China we can criticize Darwin, but not the government: in America, you can criticize the government, but not Darwin."[21]
*Chinese Paleontologist (name not disclosed by author), Expert on Cambrian fossils*

"... many of the assumptions underlying evolutionism within the various subject areas fly in the face of known scientific laws and principles in physics, chemistry and probability."[22]
*Carl Wieland, M.D., Author*

"The community of professional scientists is a reliable source for uncontroversial facts, but ... this community has a habit of stepping well outside that boundary. . . ."[23]
*Douglas Axe, Ph.D. Molecular Biologist*

"... I became a creationist as a result of reading about evolution."[24]
*A.J. Monty White, Ph.D. Gas Kinetics, Author*

"Suspicions about Darwin's theory arise for two reasons. The first: the theory makes little sense. The second: it is supported by little evidence."[25]
*David Berlinski, Ph.D. Philosopher, Mathematician*

Regarding the file drawer effect—"Scientists are rewarded when they report studies showing a widely respected theory works. They are often penalized when they report studies showing that it doesn't work. So, what does the scientist whose study doesn't work do? Experience shows that he or she tends to just file it. . . . The file drawer for evolutionary biology is enormous."[26]
*Sean McDowell, M.A. Philosophy, Theology*

"One of the major problems with the so-called theory of evolution is that the details depend on who is telling the story . . . there is not one theory of evolution, but a body of opinions, speculations and methods of interpretation of observational facts so that they fit into the philosophy of naturalism."[27]
*Keith H. Wanser, Ph.D. Matter Physics*

Regarding scientist's reluctance to publicly question Darwinian orthodoxy—"[It] reduces their chances of getting money."[28]
*Jonathan Wells, Ph.D. Religious Studies, Molecular Biology*

"Many scientists who do not believe in creation are criticizing the evolutionary model. We are thus faced with the fact that after two centuries of conjecture, a workable mechanism for evolution has not been found."[29]
*Ariel A. Roth, Ph.D. Biology*

"Materialism has a sort of insane simplicity. It has just the quality of the madman's argument; we have at once the sense of it covering everything and the sense of it leaving everything out."[30]
*G. K. Chesterton, English Author, Journalist and Philosopher*

# Cosmology, Astronomy, Big Bang, Fine-Tuned Universe

---

"It was my science that drove me to the conclusion that the world is much more complicated than can be explained by science. . . . It was only through the supernatural that I can understand the mystery of existence."[31]
*Allen Rex Sandage, Ph.D. Astronomy*

"I agree, of course, that miracles are inherently improbable—although one cannot help wondering if they are as improbable as a universe popping into existence from nothing."[32]
*John C. Lennox, Ph.D. Mathematics, Philosophy*

Regarding the mathematically intelligible universe—"The enormous usefulness of mathematics in the natural sciences is something bordering on the mysterious. . . . [T]here is no rational explanation for it. . . ."[33]
*Eugene Wigner, Nobel Laureate in Physics*

Regarding the biblical account—". . . it teaches us that the universe is relatively young, albeit with an appearance of age and maturity. . . . To those who will inevitably complain that such a view is unsophisticated, my reply is that it is certainly superior to the irrational notion that an ordered and incomprehensibly complex universe sprung by accident from nothingness and emerged by chance into the marvel it is."[34]
*John MacArthur, Theologian, Pastor, Author*

"The most incomprehensible thing about the universe is that it is comprehensible."[35]
*Albert Einstein, Ph.D. Theoretical Physics*

"... events that can be explained neither by the laws of physics nor by chance must be explained by an appeal to the intervention of an intelligent agent."[36]
*William Dembski, Ph.D. Mathematician, Philosopher*

Regarding the speculative nature of cosmology— "... cosmologists today have invented all sorts of stuff ... to make their theories work, but stuff that has never been observed. ... Things like the mysterious 'dark matter' and 'dark energy.' They have become comfortable with inventing unknowns to explain the unknown. ... But does a universe teeming with unobservable exotica really reflect reality?"[37]
*John Hartnett, Ph.D. Physics*

Regarding the scientifically accepted tenant that the universe had a beginning—"The Christian can stand confidently within biblical truth, knowing it is in line with mainstream astrophysics and cosmology. It's the atheist who feels very uncomfortable and marginalized today."[38]
*William Lane Craig, Ph.D. Philosophy, Apologetics*

"... the First and Second Laws of Thermodynamics prove as certainly as science can prove anything that the universe could not have begun itself but that it did have a beginning."[39]
*John Blanchard, Christian Theologian, Apologist, Author*

"Almost all of the great classical philosophers ... saw the origin of the universe as lying in a transcendent reality ... that the universe is not self-explanatory, and that it requires some explanation beyond itself, was something they accepted as fairly obvious."[40]
*Keith Ward, Philosopher, Theologian, Author*

"... the first actual scientific evidence that the universe had a beginning did not appear until the early 1900s. The Bible, how-

ever, has been quietly asserting that fact for millennia. It would be good if credit were given where it is due."[41]
*John C. Lennox, Ph.D. Mathematics, Philosophy*

Regarding the precise fine-tuning of many numerical physical constants required for both the universe and the earth to exist and permit life—"The impression of design is overwhelming."[42]
*Paul Davies, Ph.D. Physics, Cosmology*

Regarding the precise fine-tuning of many numerical physical constants required for both the universe and the earth to exist and permit life—"The universe is unlikely. Very unlikely. Deeply, shockingly unlikely."[43]
*Brad Lemley, Discover Magazine*

Regarding the precise fine-tuning of many numerical physical constants required for both the universe and the earth to exist and permit life—"The fine-tuning of the universe provides prima facie evidence of deistic design. . . ."[44]
*Edward Harrison, Ph.D. Astronomer and Cosmologist*

"The universe appears to have been designed by a pure mathematician."[45]
*James Jeans, Ph.D. Physicist, Astronomer, Mathematician*

# Geology, Fossils, Earth's Age

---

Regarding evidence that disproves assumed evolutionary time frames—"A number of dinosaur bones have been discovered with red blood cells including hemoglobin, and blood vessels which are still elastic. Proteins like collagen . . . have also been found. Proven decay rates rule out their survival for many millions of years."[46]
*Jonathan D. Sarfati, Ph.D. Physical Chemistry*

Regarding the age of the earth—". . . radiochemical 'clocks' are based on unprovable assumptions, which in some instances have been falsified. . . . There is not even one scientific fact that furnishes an unequivocal demonstration of great antiquity. All the data find favorable alternative explanations within a recent creation position."[47]
*George F. Howe, Ph.D. Botany*

Regarding Darwinian bias—". . . persons who doubt the basic [Darwinian] premise are by definition creationists, and hence not to be taken seriously. That there might be no reliable fossil evidence of human evolution is out of the question."[48]
*Phillip E. Johnson, Author and Professor of Law, University of California*

". . . contrary to popular belief, the eons of time provided by geology are not based upon discoveries that geologists make, but flow out of [uniformitarian] assumptions accepted within the discipline over 150 years ago . . . [i]t is rapidly becoming apparent that [these] assumptions do not match the geological observations."[49]
*Tasman Walker, Ph.D. Engineering, Geology*

Regarding the age of the Earth—"... the science is overwhelmingly in favor of an age far younger than billions of years."[50]
*Jonathan D. Sarfati, Ph.D. Physical Chemistry*

"The known fossil record fails to document a single example of [evolutionary development] accomplishing a major morphologic transition and hence offers no evidence that the gradualistic model can be valid."[51]
*Steven Stanley, Ph.D. Paleontologist*

Regarding evidence that disproves assumed evolutionary time frames—"The real shocker, a paradigm-changer, was the discovery of preserved soft, non-bony tissue from an un-fossilized T. rex bone by Dr. Mary Schweitzer. . . . Multiple individual dinosaurs . . . have now been found with non-fossilized organic remains. The evolutionary establishment has desperately tried to explain away Schweitzer's 'dangerous discovery.'"[52]
*Emil Silvestru, Ph.D. Geologist*

"In the 100 million years . . . during which vertebrates (life forms with a spinal cord or backbone) are said to have evolved from invertebrates, not one transitional form has been found."[53]
*John Blanchard, Christian Theologian, Apologist, Author*

Regarding the error of uniformitarianism in geology—"This outlook assumes and asserts that the earth's past can be correctly understood purely in terms of present-day processes acting at more or less present-day rates . . . [and] materialist geologists have assumed that the present can fully account for the earth's past. In so doing, they have been forced to ignore and suppress abundant contrary evidence that the planet has suffered major catastrophe [catastrophism] on a global scale."[54]
*John R. Baumgardner, Ph.D. Geophysics*

Regarding the fossil record—". . . one can hardly find a more factual example for the weaknesses of [the] naturalistic view, making the fossil record a true Achilles' heel of evolution. Darwin knew it, and modern paleontologists know it."[55]
*Emil Silvestru, Ph.D. Geologist*

Regarding vertical fossils—"How do you explain vertical fossilized trees or a dinosaur's neck sticking through strata that are allegedly millions of years old? There are thousands of examples. A catastrophic flood fits the evidence. . . ."[56]
*Stephen Grocott Ph.D. Organometallic Chemistry*

". . . the geologic record does not support the grand-scale evolutionary timeline."[57]
*Tasman Walker, Ph.D. Engineering, Geology*

". . . the data can be used in either direction [creation or evolution], but, since the majority of paleontologists are also evolutionists, the majority of interpretations in the field assume evolution. . . . The fossil record . . . is mainly a record of the burial of creatures during the flood. . . ."[58]
*Emil Silvestru, Ph.D. Geologist*

"At the level of kingdoms, phyla, and classes, descent with modification from common ancestors is obviously not an observed fact. To judge from the fossil and molecular evidence, it's not even a well-supported theory."[59]
*Jonathan Wells, Ph.D. Religious Studies, Molecular Biology*

"Not only do we need to reject uniformitarianism, but we also need to look at the geological evidence free of million-year-old shackles. When we do, we find the evidence is best explained by biblical history. . . . The evidence we find is what we would expect from the Bible's account of the global catastrophic Flood of Noah's day."[60]
*Tasman Walker, Ph.D. Engineering, Geologist*

"No fossil is buried with its birth certificate; the intervals of time that separate fossils are so huge that we cannot say anything definite about their possible connection through ancestry and descent."[61]
*Henry Gee, Chief Science Writer for Nature*

Regarding sedimentary deposits—"What do you see in the geology of the world? Massive sedimentary deposits. How did they form? Primarily through moving water. Belief that these formed through gradual erosion over millions of years does not fit with common sense or good science. . . . The belief that it was a little bit of water over a long time (versus a lot of water over a little bit of time) is a faith-based position that is not supported by science . . ."[62]
*Stephen Grocott, Ph.D. Organometallic Chemistry*

# Molecular Biology, Genetics, Biological Irreducible Complexity

---

"There will never, ever be a scientific explanation for mind and consciousness."[63]
*J. P. Moreland, Ph.D. Philosophy*

Regarding the limits of Darwinian evolution—". . . how many steps should we expect random mutation and natural selection to climb before getting stuck. . .? Very few. Using a sophisticated mathematical model, H. Allen Orr decided that the likeliest number for a single gene was between just one and two."[64]
*Michael J. Behe, Ph.D. Biology, Professor of Biochemistry*

"Charles Darwin knew nothing of genetics. Thus, his ideas of evolution were developed in a vacuum where speculative ideas abounded."[65]
*Robert Carter, Ph.D. Marine Biology*

Regarding the irreducible complexity of molecular life—". . . the machinery of life displays functional coherence on a scale that's presently beyond human comprehension, to say nothing of human imitation."[66]
*Douglas Axe, Ph.D. Molecular Biologist*

Regarding the irreducible complexity of molecular life—"The complexity of the simplest imaginable living organism is mind-boggling. . . . The combined telecommunications systems of the world are far less complex . . ."[67]
*Stephen Grocott Ph.D. Organometallic Chemistry*

"Even the tiniest of bacterial cells, weighing less than a trillionth of a gram, is a veritable micro miniaturized factory containing

thousands of exquisitely designed pieces of intricate molecular machinery, made up altogether of 100 thousand million atoms, far more complicated than any machine built by man and absolutely without parallel in the non-living world."[68]
*John C. Lennox, Ph.D. Mathematics, Philosophy*

"Blood coagulation is a paradigm of the staggering complexity that underlies even apparently simple bodily processes. Faced with such complexity beneath even simple phenomena, Darwinian theory falls silent . . . no one on earth has the vaguest idea how the coagulation cascade came to be."[69]
*Michael J. Behe, Ph.D. Biology, Professor of Biochemistry*

". . . it would take a minimum of a hundred years of Cray [supercomputer] time to simulate what takes place in your eye many times each second."[70]
*John Stevens, Ph.D. Professor of Physiology and Biomedical Engineering*

"The simplest organism capable of independent life . . . is a masterpiece of miniaturized complexity which makes a spaceship seem rather low tech."[71]
*Phillip E. Johnson, Author and Professor of Law, University of California*

"Mind is like no other property of physical systems. . . . It is not just that we don't know the mechanisms that give rise to it. We have difficulty in seeing how any mechanism can give rise to it."[72]
*Erich Harth, Ph.D. Physics*

"In biological organisms the smallest unit of life is the cell, and the number of parts it contains at the subatomic level is usually much larger than a trillion."[73]
*Jerry R. Bergman, Ph.D. Human Biology*

"All alleged proofs of 'evolution in action' to date do not show that functional new information is added to genes. Rather, they involve sorting and/or loss of information."[74]
*Jonathan D. Sarfati, Ph.D. Physical Chemistry*

Regarding the probability that an information-rich molecule arose by chance—". . . the chance that chance is true . . . is less than one in a trillion trillion. Some scientists use 'chance' as a catchall explanation or a cover for ignorance."[75]
*Stephen C. Meyer, Ph.D. Philosophy of Science*

". . . the findings of more than fifty years of DNA research have provided . . . a new and enormously powerful argument for design."[76]
*Anthony Flew, Ph.D. Philosophy*

". . . although it is polite and deferential, discontent with traditional Darwinism rumbles among many scientists who think most intently about evolutionary issues."[77]
*Michael J. Behe, Ph.D. Biology, Professor of Biochemistry*

# Origins, Information Science, Divine Intelligence

---

"There are various theories on the origin of life. They all run aground on this most central of central questions: 'How did the Genetic Code, along with the mechanisms for its translation, originate?'"[78]
*Douglas Hofstadter, Ph.D. Mathematics, Professor of Cognitive Science*

Regarding science creating life in the lab—"The problem is you can't make a living cell. There's not even any point in trying. It would be like a physicist doing an experiment to see if he can get a rock to fall upwards all the way to the moon. . . . The problem of assembling the right parts in the right way at the right time and at the right place, while keeping out the wrong material, is simply insurmountable."[79]
*Jonathan Wells, Ph.D. Religious Studies, Molecular Biology*

"The probability of life originating at random is so utterly miniscule as to make it absurd. . . . The only logical answer to life is creation—and not accidental random shuffling. . . . Living systems could not have been generated by random processes, within a finite time-scale, in a finite universe."[80]
*Chandra Wickramasinghe, Ph.D. Mathematics, Astronomy*

Regarding coded information in the cell—". . . the non-materiality of information points to a nonmaterial source—a mind, the mind of God."[81]
*John C. Lennox, Ph.D. Mathematics, Philosophy*

"For 150 years many scientists have insisted that 'chance and necessity'—happenstance and law—jointly suffice to explain the

origin of life on earth. We now find, however, that orthodox evolutionary thinking—with its reliance upon these twin pillars of materialistic thought—has failed to explain the origin of the central feature of living things: information." [82]
*Stephen C. Meyer, Ph.D. Philosophy of Science*

Regarding counterintuitive naturalistic assumptions—"Somehow the universe has engineered, not just its own awareness, but also its own comprehension. Mindless, blundering atoms have conspired to make not just life, not just mind, but understanding." [83]
*Paul Davies, Ph.D. Physics, Cosmology*

Regarding information in the cell—"Information is analogous to language. . . . A message requires a message sender; a book requires an author, and a program requires a programmer." [84]
*Jonathan D. Sarfati, Ph.D. Physical Chemistry*

"There is no widely accepted remotely plausible scenario for the emergence of life on earth." [85]
*David Berlinski, Ph.D. Philosopher, Mathematician*

"If science is based on experience, then science tells us that the message of encoded DNA must have originated from an intelligent cause. What kind of intelligent agent was it? On its own, science cannot answer this question; it must leave it to religion. . . . But this should not prevent science from acknowledging evidences for an intelligent cause origin wherever they exist." [86]
*Dean Kenyon, Ph.D. Biophysics*

Regarding Darwinian linguistic ambiguity—". . . no causative factors are cited. . . . [The effect] 'appears,' 'is born,' 'arises,' 'springs forth,' 'is unleashed.' What exactly, we might ask, is causing all this springing and unleashing? [This kind of] language conceals enormous difficulties." [87]
*Michael J. Behe, Ph.D. Biology, Professor of Biochemistry*

"The deeper down you probe in the ultimate nature of the structure of the universe, the more complex it becomes."[88]
*John C. Lennox, Ph.D. Mathematics, Philosophy*

". . . I do not deny that science explains, but I postulate God to explain why science explains."[89]
*Richard Swinburne, Ph.D. Philosophy*

". . . information . . . is a fundamental entity on equal footing with matter and energy . . . all living organisms are controlled by programs comprising information."[90]
*Werner Gitt, Ph.D. Engineering and Information Technology*

Regarding DNA code—"Information, not chance, is the key to life. Information is not random. . . . [It] is non-repeating, non-predictable arrangement of signals that can be read and understood by some pre-engineered system with a predetermined set of rules for storing, retrieving, and interpreting instructions. In all modern forms, information is created by an intelligent agent. . . ."[91]
*Jonathan D. Sarfati, Ph.D. Physical Chemistry*

"DNA is not a special life-giving molecule, but a genetic databank that transmits its information using a mathematical code. How did nature fabricate the world's first digital information processor—the original living cell—from the blind chaos of blundering molecules?"[92]
*Paul Davies, Ph.D. Physics, Cosmology*

"Only a rookie who knows nothing about science would say science takes away from faith. If you really study science, it will bring you closer to God."[93]
*James Tour, Ph.D. Organic Chemistry, Nano-scientist*

Regarding the real-world limits of evolution at the cellular level—"... if it can do so little, why is random mutation / natural selection so highly regarded by biologists? Because the dominant theory requires it. There is ample precedent in the history of science for the overwhelming bulk of the scientific community strongly believing in imaginary entities postulated by a favored theory."[94]
*Michael J. Behe, Ph.D. Biology, Professor of Biochemistry*

"The Origin of Life Foundation, Inc. currently offers a $1 million prize to anyone providing a chemically plausible naturalistic solution for the origin of the genetic code and life.... The problem is further from being solved than ever...."[95]
*Jonathan D. Sarfati, Ph.D. Physical Chemistry*

Regarding belief in Darwinian materialism—"... there is no rational basis for such belief. It is utter fantasy. Coded language structures are non-material in nature and absolutely require a non-material explanation"[96]
*John R. Baumgardner, Ph.D. Geophysics*

Regarding the fact that creation as well as creatures look designed—"Design inference ... does not constitute an argument from ignorance. Instead, it constitutes an 'inference to the best explanation' based upon our best available knowledge."[97]
*Stephen C. Meyer, Ph.D. Philosophy of Science*

"Christians do not believe that this universe is a closed system of cause and effect. They believe that it is open to the causal activity of its Creator-God."[98]
*John C. Lennox, Ph.D. Mathematics, Philosophy*

"It has been my experience ... that the ones who oppose the theory of design most vociferously do so for religious reasons ... they're not excited because they disagree with the science; it's

because they see the extra-scientific implications of intelligent design and they don't like where it's leading."[99]
*Michael J. Behe, Ph.D. Biology, Professor of Biochemistry*

"If you begin with an infinite mind, then you can explain how finite minds could come into existence. That makes sense. What doesn't make sense—and which many atheistic evolutionists are conceding—is the idea of getting a mind to squirt into existence by starting with brute, dead, mindless matter."[100]
*Phillip E. Johnson, Author and Professor of Law, University of California*

Regarding the claim there is exquisite design in the created order—"to counter this claim, someone would have to show that what both intuition and calculation affirm to be impossible somehow isn't impossible. Anyone not even pretending to do this hasn't understood what needs to be demonstrated. No one has said, 'Look!' We've found a way for the impossible to happen!' And if they did? Well, their demonstration would be the world's first scientifically proved, mathematically validated instance of magic."[101]
*Douglas Axe, Ph.D. Molecular Biologist*

"As a philosopher of science, I've always thought there was something odd and even disingenuous about the objection that intelligent design is not scientific. The argument shifts the focus from an interesting question of truth to a trivial question of definition.... To be a truth-seeking endeavor, the question that origin-of-life research must address is not, 'Which materialistic scenario seems most adequate?' but rather, 'What actually caused life to arise on earth?' Clearly, one possible answer to that latter question is this: 'Life was designed by an intelligent agent....'"[102]
*Stephen C. Meyer, Ph.D. Philosophy of Science*

"The difference between a late 20th century believer in the Creator God and one living in 1500 B.C., at the time of Moses, boils down to the fact that now we have a better perspective on the greatness of the Lord."[103]
*George Javor, Ph.D. Biochemistry*

"Everyone who is seriously involved in the pursuit of science becomes convinced that a spirit is manifest in the laws of the Universe—a spirit vastly superior to that of man, and one in the face of which we with our modest powers must feel humble."[104]
*Albert Einstein, Ph.D. Theoretical Physics*

"It is the sheer universality of perfection, the fact that everywhere we look, to whatever depth we look, we find an elegance and ingenuity of an absolutely transcending quality, which so mitigates against the idea of chance . . . [it] is the very antithesis of chance."[105]
*Michael Denton, Ph.D. Biologist*

"From the far reaches of the universe to the depths of the cell, separate branches of modern science have all discovered astonishing, unexpected fine-tuning—design. . . . When an Induction, obtained from one class of facts, coincides with an Induction, obtained from another different class of facts, we can be very confident it is correct."[106]
*Michael J. Behe, Ph.D. Biology, Professor of Biochemistry*

"In 1992, the historian of science Frederic Burnham said the God hypothesis is now a more respectable hypothesis than at any time in the last one hundred years. I'd go even further. More than just being respectable, I'd say that the God hypothesis is forceful enough to warrant a verdict that he's alive and well."[107]
*Stephen C. Meyer, Ph.D. Philosophy of Science*

# Notes: Chapter 6

[1] Michael Denton, *Evolution: A Theory in Crisis* (Chevy Chase, MD: Adler & Adler Pub., 1986), 46..
[2] Douglas Axe, *Undeniable* (New York, NY: Harper One, 2016), 59.
[3] Michael Behe, *The Edge of Evolution* (New York, NY; Free Press, 2008), 190.
[4] Phillip E. Johnson, *Darwin on Trial* (Downers Grove, IL: Intervarsity Press, 2010), 188, 192.
[5] Cited in Jonathan Wells, *Icons of Evolution* (Washington D.C.: Regnery Publishing, 2002), 222.
[6] Ker C. Thomson, "Geophysics," in *In Six Days: Why Fifty Scientists Choose to Believe in Creation*, (Green Forest, AR: Master Books, 2001), 217.
[7] Wells, 231.
[8] John Lennox, *God's Undertaker* (Oxford, England: Lion Books, 2009), 112.
[9] Johnson, 183.
[10] Denton, 76.
[11] Jonathan Sarfati, *The Greatest Hoax on Earth* (Atlanta, GA: Creation Book Publishers, 2010), 322.
[12] John MacArthur, *The Battle for the Beginning* (Nashville, TN: W Publishing Group, 2001), 26.
[13] John Blanchard, *Does God Believe in Atheists?* (Darlington, UK: Evangelical Press), 64.
[14] David Berlinski, *The Deniable Darwin* (Seattle, WA: Discovery Institute Press, 2009), 348.
[15] Cited in Lee Strobel, *The Case For a Creator* (Grand Rapids, MI: Zondervan, 2004), 31.
[16] John Lennox, *Seven Days That Divided The World* (Grand Rapids, MI: Zondervan, 2011), 85.
[17] Cited in Berlinski, *The Deniable Darwin*, 96.
[18] Ariel A. Roth, "Biology," in *In Six Days*, 86.
[19] Timothy Standish, "Biology," in *In Six Days*, 117.
[20] Cited in Berlinski, *The Deniable Darwin*, 348.
[21] Cited in Wells, 57-58.
[22] Carl Wieland, "Forward," in *Evolution's Achilles' Heels* (Powder Springs, GA: Creation Book Publishers, 2014), 13.
[23] Axe, 64.
[24] A. J. Monty White, "Physical Chemistry," in *In Six Days*, 260.
[25] David Berlinski, *The Devil's Delusion* (New York, NY: Basic Books, 2008), 187.
[26] Sean McDowell, *Understanding Intelligent Design* (Eugene, OR: Harvest House Pub., 2008), 77.
[27] Keith H. Wanser, "Physics," in *In Six Days*, 103.
[28] Wells, 193.
[29] Roth, "Biology," in *In Six Days*, 92.

[30] G. K. Chesterton, Orthodoxy (Mineola, NY: Dover Publications, 2004), 15.
[31] Sharon Begley, "Science Finds God," *Newsweek*, July 20, 1998.
[32] John Lennox, *God and Stephen Hawking* (Oxford, England: Lion Hudson, 2014), 90.
[33] Cited in Lennox, *God's Undertaker*, 61.
[34] MacArthur, 30.
[35] Cited in Lennox, *God's Undertaker*, 59.
[36] Cited in Berlinski, *The Deniable Darwin*, 301.
[37] John Hartnett, "Cosmology," in *Evolution's Achilles' Heels*, 222.
[38] Cited in Strobel, 121.
[39] Blanchard, 58.
[40] Cited in Lennox, *God's Undertaker*, 47.
[41] Lennox, *God and Stephen Hawking*, 46.
[42] Paul Davies, *The Cosmic Blueprint* (New York, NY: Simon and Schuster, 1988), 203.
[43] Brad Lemley, "Why Is There Life?" *Discover Magazine*.com, November 1, 2000, accessed May 15, 2018. http://discovermagazine.com/2000/nov/cover/.
[44] Edward Harrison, *Masks of the Universe* (New York, NY: Macmillian, 1985) 252, 263.
[45] Cited in Paul Davies, *The Goldilocks Enigma* (Great Britain: The Penguin Press, 20116), 8.
[46] Sarfati, *The Greatest Hoax on Earth*, 203.
[47] George F. Howe, "Botany," in *In Six Days*, 255-256.
[48] Johnson, 108.
[49] Tasman Walker, "The Geological Record," in *Evolution's Achilles' Heels*, 156.
[50] Sarfati, *The Greatest Hoax on Earth*, 203.
[51] Cited in Blanchard, 96.
[52] Emil Silvestru, "The Fossil Record," in *Evolution's Achilles' Heels*, 129.
[53] Blanchard, 96.
[54] John R. Baumgardner, "Geophysics," in *In Six Days*, 230-231.
[55] Silvestru, in *Evolution's Achilles' Heels*, 113.
[56] Stephen Grocott, "Inorganic Chemistry," in *In Six Days*, 151.
[57] Walker, in *Evolution's Achilles' Heels*, 191.
[58] Silvestru, in *Evolution's Achilles' Heels*, 116.
[59] Wells, 57.
[60] Walker, in *Evolution's Achilles' Heels*, 182.
[61] Cited in Wells, 220.
[62] Grocott, *In Six Days*, 150-151.
[63] Cited in Strobel, 268.
[64] Behe, *The Edge of Evolution*, 116.
[65] Robert Carter, "Genetics and DNA," in *Evolution's Achilles' Heels*, 50.
[66] Axe, 166.
[67] Grocott, *In Six Days*, 149.
[68] Lennox, *God's Undertaker*, 122.
[69] Michael Behe, *Darwin's Black Box*, (New York, NY: Touchstone, 1996), 97.

[70] Cited in Sarfati, *The Greatest Hoax on Earth*, 274.
[71] Johnson, 133.
[72] Cited in Berlinski, *The Devil's Delusion*, 175.
[73] Jerry R. Bergman, "Biology," in *In Six Days*, 25.
[74] Sarfati, *The Greatest Hoax on Earth*, 44.
[75] Steven Meyer, *Signature in the Cell* (New York, NY: Harper Collins Publishers, 2010), 222, 223.
[76] Cited in Sarfati, "The Origin of Life," in *Evolution's Achilles' Heels*, 82.
[77] Behe, *The Edge of Evolution*, 190.
[78] Cited in Lennox, *God's Undertaker*, 122.
[79] Cited in Strobel, 39.
[80] Cited in Blanchard, 298.
[81] Lennox, *Seven Days That Divide The World*, 101.
[82] Meyer, 451.
[83] Davies, *The Goldilocks Enigma*, 5.
[84] Sarfati, *The Greatest Hoax on Earth*, 225-226.
[85] Berlinski, *The Deniable Darwin*, 126.
[86] Cited in Lennox, *God's Undertaker*, 187.
[87] Behe, *Darwin's Black Box*, 93-94.
[88] Lennox, *God's Undertaker*, 179.
[89] Cited in Lennox, *God's Undertaker*, 47.
[90] Werner Gitt, *In the Beginning Was Information* (Green Forest, AR: Master Books, 2006), 11.
[91] Sarfati, in *Evolution's Achilles' Heels*, 85.
[92] Paul Davies, "Paul Davies: How We Could Create Life," *The Guardian*, 11 December 2002, accessed April 27, 2018, http://www.guardian.co.uk/education/2002/dec/11/highereducation.uk.
[93] Candace Adams, "Leading Nano-scientist Builds Big Faith," *The Baptist Standard*, March 15, 2002.
[94] Behe, *The Edge of Evolution*, 163.
[95] Sarfati, *The Greatest Hoax on Earth*, 247.
[96] Baumgardner, *In Six Days*, 230.
[97] Meyer, 377.
[98] Lennox, *God and Stephen Hawking*, 88.
[99] Cited in Strobel, 215.
[100] Cited in Strobel, 264.
[101] Axe, 198.
[102] Meyer, 399, 437.
[103] George Javor, "Biochemistry," in *In Six Days*, 137.
[104] Cited in John Lennox, *Gunning For God* (Oxford, England: Lion Books, 2011), 48.
[105] Denton, 342.
[106] Behe, *The Edge of Evolution*, 219.
[107] Cited in Strobel, 84.

# ~seven~

## Empirical God

"And when we look at the evidence . . . from cosmology, physics, biology, and human consciousness, we find that theism has amazing explanatory scope and power. The existence of God explains this broad range of evidence more simply, adequately, and comprehensively than any other worldview. . . ."[1]
*Stephen C. Meyer, Ph.D. Philosophy of Science*

". . . what looks to be the fruit of genius always is the fruit of genius . . . our firm sense that certain things can't happen by accident is absolutely correct."[2]
*Douglas Axe, Ph.D. Molecular Biologist*

"Although the biblical account clashes at many points with the naturalistic and evolutionary hypothesis, it is not in conflict with a single scientific fact. Indeed, all the geological, astronomical, and scientific data can be easily reconciled to the biblical account."[3]
*John MacArthur, Theologian, Pastor, Author*

"Sir Isaac Newton . . . [wrote] *Principia Mathematica,* the most famous book in the history of science, expressing the hope that it would 'persuade the thinking man' to believe in God."[4]
*John C. Lennox, Ph.D. Mathematics, Philosophy*

I didn't know I could believe more. But I do.

It is the wholly unexpected consequence of immersing myself in the scientific minutiae of creation. I wrote this book to expose Darwin not to intensify my faith. But that is what God has done in me through this process. It's a bit startling and somewhat difficult to explain. It's my hope that in writing this concluding chapter, I will figure out how to say it.

I've been a Christian since 1983 and I've truly believed. I mean, I've really believed. My whole life has been turned upside down because I've believed. I won't bore you with the details, but I was once a mild-mannered, middle-aged accountant living in Little Rock, Arkansas. Now, I'm a highly excitable preacher who has lived in Milan, Italy, since 2003. I just want you to understand that I've believed with all of my life. I tell you this only to emphasize the fact that today, after writing this book, I believe more. These gifted scientists and scholars I've been reading and quoting are culpable in this. Their descriptions of what the data is revealing have had one principal effect on me—worship! You know, the deep wonderment, awe, fear, and trembling kind of worship. Writing this book has been a very close encounter of the divine kind in a brand-new sphere—as an eyewitness in the physical realm. This enhanced glimpse of my Creator has been life altering, as all true encounters with Him are. Indeed, He is the empirical God! I believe more!

## Empirical Faith

Since my conversion at the age of twenty-eight, I have believed, and known, and proclaimed that Jesus Christ is God. I have believed it, and have known it, biblically, theologically, historically, spiritually, intellectually, logically, rationally, emotionally, experientially, and personally. I have believed it and have known it more than I have believed and known anything else in my life. Again, I've staked everything upon who He is, what He's said, and what He's done. Yet, through my research for this book and its writing, I've believe in a whole new kind of way. I now believe in a more exhaustive empirical sense.

> **Empirical 1. a.** Relying upon or derived from observation or experiment: **b.** Capable of proof or verification by means of observation or experiment. **2.** Relying solely on practical experience and without regard for system or theory.[5]

While one cannot fail to rationally, logically, and compellingly infer God from simply looking around, He has left His indelible and observable autograph on the exquisite nanotechnology within the cell. Again, it's "His signature,"[6] as Ph.D. Stephen Meyer has eloquently and exhaustively demonstrated in his 600-page treatise on DNA. It's not that I ever doubted God was there; it's that now—I can never doubt that God is there! I've seen His fingerprint! You can't look at the "verification and observable proof of" infinite intellect within the cell and not comprehend that He has left undeniable evidence of His presence.

For the thinking person, this is "practical experience without regard for system or theory." With the discovery of the indefinable complexity, volumes of coded genetic information, and irreducible engineering intricacies at the molecular level, science has proven beyond any reasonable doubt that there is a Genius-Creator. No unbiased person can read the data in any other conceivable way. All attempts to account for the 3.5 billion base pairs of algorithmic code in human DNA from strictly natural or materialistic processes are transparently preposterous—exhausting, as noted in chapter five, the probabilistic resources of the known Universe!

## Brute Reason

As I was looking at my Creator's autograph in the double helix of the DNA molecule and reading about its manifold marvels and capacities, there was something *after* reflexive worship. Beyond worship, there is inescapable brute reason. Even the open, clear-thinking, unregenerate mind can see it. Genius-Creator is there. Or, I guess I should say, here. He really is inescapably here. So, if we're starting at zero, meaning, before any supernatural revelation, the ensuing question rationally follows. Who is He? Who is this Infinite Intellect? In answer, I think the logical first step is to acknowledge that we only have two plausible choices. The Creator is either an unrevealed, unknown deist god, or, the God of the Bible. I single out the God of the Bible because there simply are no other intelligible God-revelations in the world.

Accordingly, it seems the second logical step would be to look at the evidence for the God of the Bible. To succinctly consummate this line of thinking, please allow me to coattail on C. S. Lewis' critique of the worldview he called the "Scientific Outlook."[7] He first critiques scientism and then reasons his way to the God of the Bible, Jesus Christ. He writes that . . .

> emergent evolution . . . seems to be a pure hallucination . . . whatever else may be true, the popular scientific cosmology at any rate is certainly not. I left that ship . . . because I thought it could not keep afloat. Something like philosophical idealism or Theism must, at the very worst, be less untrue than that. And idealism turned out, when you took it seriously, to be disguised Theism. And once you accepted Theism, you could not ignore the claims of Christ. And when you examined them it appeared to me that you could adopt no middle position. Either He was a lunatic, or God. And He was not a lunatic.[8]

It seems to me we are left with a very simple choice. An unrevealed-theoretical-shot-in-the-dark, reclusive-anthropophobiac, deist god, or, the historically and scripturally revealed God of the Bible. Renown eighteenth-century theologian Jonathan Edwards logically argued, as twentieth-century theologian John Gerstner writes, "that if there is a God, He would reveal Himself and that the Bible is the only such revelation."[9] For indeed, as Lewis emphasized, Jesus Christ is God, or He is a lunatic, and He is no lunatic. So yes, the thinking person will rationally deduce the deity of Jesus Christ or dodge the logical dictates of his mind in favor of some fugitive, cartoon-god. Christ's birth, His life, His words, His deeds, His death, and His resurrection not only fulfilled all the Old Testament prophecies regarding Messiah, but they also self-evidently confirm His divinity to any reasonable person. Jesus Christ is the Genius-Creator! It's His *"Signature in the cell!"*

### It's Not That Men Don't Know, It's That They Do

Of course, every born-again believer understands that true Christian conversion transcends mere rationality, but it in no way conflicts with rationality. Given the evidence, it's not that every human being couldn't reason his way to the obvious deity of Jesus Christ. No, it's not that he couldn't do it. It's that he doesn't want to do it. He has no interest in doing it. Christianity is not ultimately an intellectual question, although it is, in fact, intellectually appealing, convincing, and satisfying. Christianity is finally a moral question. It's not that men don't know, it's that they do. It's always Romans Chapter One. Men. . .

> . . . suppress the truth in unrighteousness, because that which is known about God is evident within them; for God made it evident to them. For since the creation of the world His invisible attributes, His eternal power and divine nature have been clearly seen being understood through what has been made, so that they are without excuse. For even though they knew God, they did not honor

> Him as God, or give thanks, but they became futile in their speculations, and their foolish heart was darkened. Professing to be wise, they became fools. . . .[10]

You might be a liar but you're not an atheist or even agnostic. God's Word says you instinctively, intuitively, and viscerally know you have a Creator. We all know. The book of God's works reveals His necessary presence and the book of His word reveals His unquestioned identity. And by His overwhelming revelation—without and within—we know His name. It's Jesus Christ. As noted, in researching for this book and never getting to the end of the "clearly seen" glory of God in creation, I have repeatedly been thrust into a kind of worship of self-defense. I guess what I mean is that worship was the only thing left for me to do. There were, and are, no other viable options in the face of His "invisible attributes, eternal power, and divine nature."[11] I *had* to worship—not in an obligatory sense, but in an I-*had*-to-worship sense! You know, in a try-and-stop-me-from-worshiping kind of way! There is just too much awe! A very real and very present awe of the very real and very present God!

## We're Supposed to Be in Awe

This whole empirical thing has just taken me to an entirely new place with God—a richer place. When I meditate deeply upon His fingerprints everywhere evident in creation, from the "deep space field"[12] to DNA, I am immediately affected in an extraordinarily powerful way. There is just more awe. More wonder. More astonishment. More mindfulness. More humility. More contrition. More repentance. More reverence. More joy. More faith. More ardor. More resolve. More anticipation. More worship. I mean, the DNA thing alone is intensely worship-provoking. I do so love His undeniable autograph in the cell! I didn't need it. But I love it! I was a fully persuaded lover and follower of Jesus Christ before I got ear-deep into the data but now there's more—there's just a whole lot more! I'm pretty sure this is how God intended for it to be. Creation should affect us like this. We're supposed to be in awe! Like the angels are! For at God's creative fiat "... the morning stars sang together, and all the sons of God shouted for joy!"[13] It's what is happening in my heart as I contemplate my own "observable and verifiable" "createdness."

Yeah, Satan knows what he's doing in attacking what Francis Schaffer calls "the createdness of things."[14] He seeks to obscure the clear fingerprint of God in the eyes of fallen man with his patently absurd, but all-too-willingly-believed theories of Big Bang and Darwinian evolution. Without "createdness" all we have left is "uncreatedness"[15] which, as noted in Chapter One, means, "not that something does not exist, but that it just stands there, autonomous to itself, without solutions and without answers."[16] This is modern man's most urgent problem. Twenty-first-century man needs a strong, sobering, arresting prescription of "createdness"—without which, yes, of course, humanity just stands there, "without solutions and without answers."

## A Huge Dose of "Createdness"

You may recall, there's a man in the Bible who was in search of some answers. His name was Job. Remember what he got? A huge dose of "createdness." It's what Job needed more than anything else. Job was a righteous man who believed in God but in his trauma, he obviously needed more clarity on the "createdness" thing. It will change everything for him, just like it does for you and me. Job has a few questions. But God doesn't come to Job answering questions; He comes asking them. God does not explain Himself to Job, or to any other man, but He does graciously reveal the unalterable implications of "createdness." God comes to Job to help him get the whole Creator-creature dynamic sorted out. Just a few selected verses ...

> Then the LORD answered Job out of the whirlwind and said, "Who is this that darkens counsel by words without

> knowledge? Now gird your loins like a man, and I will ask you, and you instruct Me! Where were you when I laid the foundation of the earth? Tell Me, if you have understanding. . . . Have you ever in your life commanded the morning and caused the dawn to know its place. . . ? Have you entered into the springs of the sea or walked in the recesses of the deep. . . ? Have you understood the expanse of the earth. . . ? Where is the way to the dwelling of light. . .? Can you bind the Pleiades, or loose the cords of Orion? Can you lead forth a constellation in its season. . . ? Do you know the ordinances of the heavens, or fix their rule over the earth. . . ? Can you send forth lightnings that they may go and say to you, here we are. . . ? Do you give the horse his might? Do you clothe his neck with a mane. . . ? Is it by your understanding that the hawk soars. . . ? Is it at your command that the eagle mounts up and makes his nest on high?"[17]

## You're God, I'm Not

God comes with seventy such questions, and what was Job's response to Yahweh's "createdness" tutorial? Perfect, complete and utter humility, contrition, and repentance—with, it should be noted, at least one hand over his mouth. In effect, Job says, "I'm going to shut up now—You're God, I'm not."[18] His response was the response of any sane human being when confronted with the overwhelming evidence of God's genius and, by comparison, the underwhelming limitations of our two-and-a-half pounds of grey matter. It's the response that pseudoscience has attempted to steal from mankind. Big Bang and Darwinian evolutionary theory inevitably seek to excise submissiveness before the Transcendent out of the human experience. There is no humility, contrition, and repentance in the face of "uncreatedness." There is only arrogance and an inevitable self-destructive kind of nihilism. Darwinism is the unparalleled tragedy of mankind in the last 150 years. Ideologies that embraced it largely account for the blood bath that was the twentieth century. The "uncreatedness" presupposition of scientism is lethal both in this life and the next. Apart from acknowledging our "createdness" we are doomed to a joyless, and finally, meaningless temporal life—and then, an unspeakably terrifying eternity. Yes, the Apostle is right about fallen man and his "uncreatedness" theorems. "Professing to be wise, they became fools."[19]

## The Empirical God Effect

"Createdness" is the worst thing you can take from a human being. We are less than a mere shadow of what we were created to be without our awareness of our empirical Creator. If He is irrefutably here, and He is, He changes everything every day for the true believer! His firsthand presence radically alters our perspective on every last issue we encounter. If you are profoundly aware of your "createdness" and its stunning implications, you can't perpetually obsess over the minutiae of life. You simply won't do it. With the empirical God in view, all things quite naturally come into proper focus. You will not be excessively preoccupied with the temporal when considering His objective, palpable certainty. You can't be. I challenge you to try to agonize, fret, and stew about some worldly issue while genuinely meditating on the very immediate reality of His "hereness." You can't. Biblically accurate contemplation of the empirical God will make you and all your anxieties just the right size—meaning awed worship of a breathtaking God takes precedence at every turn, every day, in every circumstance.

Moreover, in the face of the verified God, the thinking person cannot continue to be arrogant, prideful, obstinate, self-absorbed, worried, and unrepentant. You simply cannot ignore empirical God, the right-here God. You cannot be indifferent toward Him. You cannot be unmoved when mindful of His powerful, tangible presence. You cannot disregard His Word. You cannot sin with impunity. You cannot. You will not, if you're truly grasping His "hereness." That indeed, He is in every way more real and more here than this book you're reading. The Apostle said it like this: ". . . in Him we live and move and exist."[20] If we intellectually own this, as any rational person must, we will have the appropriate sense of His nearness and a proper fear of Him who grants our next heartbeat. We will be humble before Him. We will be profoundly convinced of our "createdness." Consequently, we will see every issue through the lens of His stunning "Godness." To fear the discernable God is, as the wise king writes, "the beginning of knowledge . . . and wisdom."[21] Only the fool ignores Solomon's counsel on this point.

## Just Plain Old Scary Stupid

Bible-believing Christians know a truth war began in the Garden. It still rages. The "father of lies"[22] just keeps lying about everything—particularly "createdness." He is no doubt especially proud of Big Bang and Darwinism. Incredibly, Satan has much of mankind believing, as Lee Strobel writes, that "nothing produces everything, non-life produces life, randomness produces fine-tuning, chaos produces information, unconsciousness produces consciousness, non-reason produces reason."[23] I know. When you write it out like that it's just plain old scary stupid. This is the degree to which fallen man is predisposed to embrace any lie that gives him license. No lie, it seems, is too idiotic to reject if it assists in humanity's unending declaration of independence from the Creator-God. It's true, Big Bang and Darwinism are the greatest engines of atheism in the history of man. Yeah, you can almost hear Satan laughing.

## The Triumph of Ideology Over Common Sense

Obviously, any goofy old lie will do. To wit, the American Association of Biology Teachers states:

> The diversity of life on earth is the outcome of evolution: an unsupervised, impersonal, unpredictable and natural process of temporal descent with genetic modification that

is affected by natural selection, chance, historical contingencies and changing environments.[24]

As we've argued, this is not true science. It is authoritarian science. It is agenda science. It's edict science. It's consensus science. It's metaphysics. It is ideology. It is naturalism. It is materialism. It is scientism. It is faith, creed, and dogma. It is the state religion. It is, as even atheist Thomas Nagel acknowledges, ". . . a heroic triumph of ideological theory over common sense."[25]

It is the ludicrous "uncreatedness" lie that consigns its adherents to a base and dismal view of life. This is what the world is teaching its children. It is a tragedy of unspeakable proportions. To quote Ph.D. Douglas Axe again, "Heroes are badly needed" in this fight, and, he adds, you don't "need to have Ph.Ds."[26] All you need is a little common sense, a very general understanding of the facts, and a willingness to speak. It's what real Christians have always done—to speak truth in the face of every last lie. Everything is at stake in the "createdness" debate. Everything.

## Scientific Truth Destroys the Root Assertion of Darwin

As we've seen, true science destroys the root assertion of Darwin. The hard fact is, as noted in Chapter Five, mankind is not evolving. Mankind is devolving. The human genome is in meltdown mode. I often hear materialists mockingly chide God for a "faulty design" because an estimated 99 percent of all species to ever live have gone extinct. Again, as Ph.D. geneticist John Sanford states, real-world mutation rates are "relentless and [are] destroying us, not creating us. We are headed for extinction, along with every other complex organism."[27] Contrary to the purveyors of scientism in this post-truth age, we are not getting better. We're on the way out. We are not moving toward greater and greater physiological development and, by extension, the ultimate societal utopia. We are dying. As every Bible-believer knows, these are our "wages."[28] To the God-mockers, it must be said that extinction and death don't have anything to do with a faulty design but have everything to do with a perfect judgment. Through God's righteous judgment of rebellious man, the whole created order has been "subjected to futility."[29] Lethal, unremitting devolution is the irrevocable diagnosis of this world and our species.

## Scientific Truth Exposes the Conspicuous Deficiencies of Darwin

Additionally, truth clearly reveals, as referenced in Chapter Four, that the evolutionary narrative doesn't begin to coherently address three fundamental and unavoidable questions about life.

- *One*: The life from non-life question. How could it have possibly ever happened? It couldn't. Any unbiased scientist will own it. To advocate otherwise is to violate a fundamental law of biology known as biogenesis, namely, that life only comes from life. Chemicals, matter, and physics do not procreate.
- *Two*: Where did the coded information in DNA come from? How could inert chemicals, enzymes, and amino acids have written their own code? They couldn't. Any unprejudiced scientist will own it. To advocate otherwise violently assaults common sense and the universal understanding that information only has one source—a Mind.
- *Three*: How did irreducibly complex, mutually dependent biological systems arise in a gradual step-by-step chance process? They couldn't. Any fair-minded scientist will own it. The odds exhaust the probabilistic resources of the known Universe!

These three arguments alone validate the Intelligent Design hypothesis and invalidate materialistic speculations. Yes, a Genius Creator-God is here. To advocate otherwise is to invoke unquantifiable naturalistic miracles, upon unquantifiable naturalistic miracles, upon unquantifiable naturalistic miracles, upon

. . . well, you get the picture. Darwin's theory is dead, and well-informed people know it. Only the obstinate Darwinian fundamentalist will not repent.

## Scientific Truth Points to the Supreme Reality of Creation

How do we answer the age-old question inquisitive men have always posed—namely, why is there something rather than nothing? Regarding the universe, renown physicist Stephen Hawking wanted to know "why it is as it is, and why it exists at all."[30] Theologian John Piper gives the ultimate answer—a worship-provoking response that satisfies the heart, soul, and mind of thinking people. He writes . . .

> In creation God went public with the glory that reverberates joyfully between the Father and the Son! There is something about the fullness of God's joy that inclines it to overflow. There is an expansive quality to His joy. . . . God loves to behold His glory reflected in His works. So, the eternal happiness of the triune God spilled over in the work of creation. This is why God has done all things, from creation to consummation, for the preservation and display of His glory. All His works are simply the spillover of his infinite exuberance for his own excellence.[31]

Yeah, if we're paying much attention at all we've sensed, seen, tasted, and touched His infinite exuberance. Even on this fallen, condemned planet, His glory inhabits our habitat. We encounter it at every turn. Jill Nelson elucidates this point perfectly . . .

> When you see a beautiful fish, God is showing you a little bit of His glory. When you pick up and feel a rock, God is showing you a little bit of His glory. When you bite into an apple and taste it, God is showing you a little bit of His

> glory. Flowers, waves, mountains, volcanoes, waterfalls, birds, giraffes, elephants, trees, bananas, pumpkins, clouds, lightning, snow, dandelions—all show us a little bit of God's greatness and worth.[32]

Is Nelson right in echoing King David's Psalm 29:9 sentiment? Does everything say glory? Yes! Yes! And yes! His glory engulfs and envelopes His creation. Only the willfully blind do not see it. Praise God, He has gone public! For indeed, His infinite-exuberant glory is the supreme delight and consummate joy of true believers! Not only in this life, but for the next billion eternities!

Christian, you know this is true. You've encountered the traces of His glory in everyday things. As sixteenth-century theologian John Calvin wrote, "There is not one little blade of grass, there is no color in this world that is not intended to make men rejoice."[33] Yesterday, I ate a few pieces of a perfect pineapple and was irresistibly drawn into worship. It looked so peculiar, like an organic piece of art. Then I bit into it. And it was like a little bit of glory dancing on my taste buds! Yum! God's tropical masterpiece was a modest but very real encounter with His infinite exuberance and grandeur!

Christian, you must be in the world telling this. You must be a hero! And as Axe reminds us, you don't need a Ph.D.! It's just "common science,"[34] "knowledge ... gained through experience."[35] You must proclaim the evident glory of the empirical God in the created order. It's what God has left you on the planet to do—to be His witness. First, by becoming informed. Then speaking, conversing, teaching, advocating. Call the lie a lie! Back to hell with every last one of them. Be bold. Never be intimidated again. Christian, we have the data! We have the science! God is calling us to wield it! Humanity desperately needs the truth of "createdness." It's essential. It's urgently necessary every day we roll out of bed. Christian, this is not optional. You must speak!

Our hearts, our souls, our minds, and our imaginations crave "infinite exuberance." The empirical God has "set eternity in [our] hearts."[36] We were made "through Him and for Him."[37] We need Him. We must have Him and every last implication of "createdness." We've been wired for the transcendent beauty, intimacy, and adventure of walking with our Genius Creator-God, Jesus Christ. For all of creation is, as C. S. Lewis writes, "a message [whereby] we know we are being touched by a finger of that right hand at which there are pleasures for evermore."[38]

In Psalm 29, David is watching a thunderstorm pass through Lebanon, and worship is rising in his heart and mind. It's the thinking person's reflexive response to the genius, power, complexity, symmetry, beauty, design, and scale revealed in the created order.

> Ascribe to the LORD glory and strength. Ascribe to the LORD the glory due to His name. . . . The God of glory thunders. . . . The voice of the LORD is powerful. The voice of the LORD is majestic. The voice of the LORD breaks the cedars. . . . The voice of the LORD hews out flames of fire. The voice of the LORD shakes the wilderness. . . .[39]

David sees it. He feels it. He knows it. It's unmistakable. There's glory. There's wonder. There's awe. There is a deep, visceral awareness of the Transcendent. His soul is shouting, *"God!"* Every true believer understands. And we "greatly rejoice with joy inexpressible"[40] as we join with our legendary Hebrew brother in heartily proclaiming his empirically true lyrics, "Everything says, 'Glory!'"

* * *

"God made the world that He might communicate, and the creature receive, His glory; and that it might be received both by the mind and heart."[41]
*Jonathan Edwards, Theologian*

"For from Him and through Him and to Him are all things. To Him be the glory forever. Amen."[42]
*Paul, God's Apostle*

# Notes: Chapter 7

[1] Cited in Lee Strobel, *The Case For a Creator* (Grand Rapids, MI: Zondervan, 2004), 83.
[2] Douglas Axe, *Undeniable* (New York, NY: Harper One, 2016), 136, 152.
[3] John MacArthur, *The Battle for the Beginning* (Nashville, TN: W Publishing Group, 2001), 28.
[4] John Lennox, *God and Stephen Hawking* (Oxford, England: Lion Hudson, 2014), 37.
[5] "Empirical," *The American Heritage Dictionary* (Boston: Houghton Mifflin Co., 1985).
[6] Steven Meyer, *Signature in the Cell* (New York, NY: Harper Collins Publishers, 2010).
[7] C. S. Lewis, *The Weight of Glory* (New York, NY: Harper Collins Publishers, 2001), 123.
[8] Ibid., 138.
[9] John Gerstner, *The Rationale of Hell* (Internet Article - https://www.the-highway.com/hell1_Gerstner.html).
[10] Romans 1:18-22.
[11] Ibid.
[12] William R. Newcott, *Hubble's Eye on the Universe* (National Geographic, April,1997), 10-11.
[13] Job 38:7.
[14] Francis Schaeffer, *Genesis in Space and Time* (Downers Grove, IL: InterVarsity Press, 1972), 30.
[15] Ibid.
[16] Ibid.
[17] Job 38:1–39:27, (Excerpts).
[18] Job 40:4-5. Author's paraphrase.
[19] Romans 1:22.
[20] Acts 17:28.
[21] Proverbs 1:7, 9:10.
[22] John 8:44.
[23] Strobel, 277.
[24] Cited by George Hawke, "Meteorology," in *In Six Days: Why Fifty Scientists Choose to Believe in Creation*, (Green Forest, AR: Master Books, 2001), 348.
[25] Thomas Nagel, *Mind & Cosmos* (New York, NY: Oxford University Press, 2012), 128.
[26] Axe, 55.
[27] Cited in Donald Batten, "Natural Selection," in *Evolutions Achilles Heels*, (Powder Springs, GA: Creation Books, 2014), 39.
[28] Romans 6:23.
[29] Romans 8:20.
[30] "Stephen Hawking Quotes." BrainyQuote. Accessed April 24, 2018. http://www.brainyquote.com/quotes/stephen_hawking_124516.
[31] John Piper, *Desiring God* (Portland, OR: Multnomah Books, 1986), 33.

[32] Jill Nelson, The ABC's of God. A Study for Children on the Greatness and Worth of God (Minneapolis, MN: Desiring God Ministries, 1999), 23.
[33] John Calvin, Sermon No. 10 on 1 Corinthians, quoted in William J. Bouwsma, *John Calvin: A Sixteenth-Century Portrait* (New York: Oxford University Press, 1988), 134-35.
[34] Axe, 10.
[35] "Science," *The American Heritage Dictionary* (Boston: Houghton Mifflin Co., 1985).
[36] Ecclesiastes 3:11.
[37] Colossians 1:16.
[38] C. S. Lewis, *Letters to Malcolm, A Mind Awake: An Anthology of C. S. Lewis*, ed. Clyde Kilby (New York: Harcourt, Brace and World, 1968), 204.
[39] Psalm 29:1-8, (Excerpts).
[40] 1 Peter 1:8.
[41] Cited in John Piper, *God's Passion for His Glory* (Wheaton, IL: Crossway Books, 1998), 79.
[42] Romans 11:36.

# ~epilogue~

## Answering God's Accusers

"I am the LORD, and there is no other; Besides Me there is no God . . . there is no one besides Me. I am the LORD and there is no other. The One forming light and creating darkness, causing well-being and creating calamity; I am the LORD who does all these. . . . Woe to the one who quarrels with his Maker—an earthenware vessel among the vessels of earth! Will the clay say to the potter, 'What are you doing?'"[1]

*Isaiah, God's Prophet*

We all know the difference between an honest question and a backhanded accusation. Regarding God and His "ways"[2] in the world, I've encountered far more of the latter in my three decades of ministry. You can always tell. It's in the tone. The inquiry will have that unmistakable air of both judging God and knowing better than He does all at the same time. The smugness and self-congratulatory arrogance are always thick, and more than a bit nauseating.

## What About the Tsunami?

So, when you write a book about creation entitled, "Everything says, 'Glory'!" you know it's coming. You know the God-accusers are poised and ready with their simplistic assessments and superficial queries. While there are several grammatical subjects I could use in the following sentence, I will employ one that I have some personal experience with. The inevitable question comes: If everything in the created order says glory, what about the tsunami? How does the tsunami say, "Glory!"?

It was December 26, 2004. My wife and I were on holiday in the States. A 9.0 earthquake in the Indian Ocean generated a 100-foot wall of water that slammed into Indonesia and fourteen other counties killing over 250,000 people—obviously, just a stunning, breathtaking calamity. Our personal connection was a young Indonesian man named Leslie who had been in our church in Milan, Italy, during 2004. We had grown to dearly love this delightful young disciple of Christ. Upon hearing the news, we repeatedly tried to contact him by email, but with no success. It wasn't until late February that he was finally able to respond—thankfully, he and his family were not directly affected.

## The God Critique Tsunami

Predictably, the God accusations began. The complaints against God were just another kind of tsunami. Amateur theologians were awash with God critiques. Where was He? Why did He let this happen? Couldn't He have stopped this? If God were good, He would have prevented this. If God were omnipotent, He would have checked it. To the pseudo-Christian, nominally religious, and to the secularist, an incident like this seems to confirm that God is either not there, not good, or not almighty. About the only time the Biblical God gets any appreciable airtime in our culture is in the aftermath of such an event when He is, in the very least, questioned, but most commonly dismissed, mocked, slandered, and indicted.

So, how does the tsunami with a quarter of a million dead say "Glory!"? Does God's Word speak to such matters? As I heard one God-accuser state, ". . . if God is the intelligent designer, He has something to answer for." Is God's design faulty? Is He an incompetent Creator? Is He powerful enough to speak a two-trillion galaxy cosmos into existence but not powerful enough to stop that quake and its wave?

Does the Bible speak to this? Does the biblically literate Christian have anything meaningful, cogent, and coherent to say in the face of such jaw-dropping, cataclysmic, natural upheaval? I would assert that the Bible-believing Christian is the only person on the planet with anything pertinent to say. And as God's people, we must speak His truth whether anyone wants to hear it or not. Unfortunately, as every genuine Christian has experienced countless times, most do not want to hear it.

## No Rogue Molecules

Sadly, if we're paying attention at all, we're cognizant that much of what is called the modern Christian church has, to varying degrees, abandoned the biblical revelation of the absolute sovereignty of God. It's as if the modern expositor feels the need, in a word, to shield God from His own self-declared dominion over all things. Obviously, this is a tragic mistake. Ultimately, God's supreme rule in every aspect of life is our only true anchor. If He is not sovereign, we are all subject to the vagaries of randomness and happenstance. One rogue molecule is all it would take to disrupt the whole created order. But Bible-believers know, there is no such particle in heaven or earth. Our God reigns! So, the first attribute of God to note in this discussion is that the tsunami is not beyond, or outside, the absolute sovereign control of Yahweh.

Just a quick survey of some of what God reveals about His sovereignty in the Bible. David proclaims, "Yours, O LORD, is the greatness and the power and the glory and the victory and the majesty, indeed everything that is in the heavens and the earth; Yours is the dominion, O LORD, and you exalt Yourself as head over all. . . . The LORD has established His throne in the heavens; and His sovereignty rules over all."[3] Daniel wrote that God ". . . does according to His will in the host of heaven and among the inhabitants of earth and no one can ward off His hand."[4] Isaiah says, "For the LORD of hosts has planned and who can frustrate it? And as for His stretched-out hand, who can turn it back?"[5] Paul reminds us that God "works all things after the counsel of His will [and] is the only Sovereign, the King of Kings and Lord of lords who alone possesses . . . eternal dominion."[6] John explodes in doxology: "Hallelujah! For the Lord our God, the Almighty, reigns."[7] El-Shaddai is the unassailable, unstoppable God who will exercise His Creator-rights in His cosmos. And lest God be a liar, that would include the falling of a sparrow,[8] the casting of dice,[9] and every last wave.[10] The prophet is right and God unapologetic, "If a calamity occurs in a city has not the LORD done it?"[11]

## Exploding Trivial Notions

Regrettably, many modern pulpits have devolved into broadcasting warm, fuzzy half-truths and sentimental clichés about the God of Scripture. By the time your average preacher gets through, God seems like a hapless, inept, effeminate, want-to-be god as opposed to the awesome, fearsome, consuming-fire God He reveals Himself to be in the Bible. Although you didn't hear it here first, there will be much wrath—starting in many pulpits and so-called churches! Regarding this chatty, breezy, user-friendly style of preaching and its rancid fruit, American theologian John Piper writes . . .

> Against the overwhelming weight and seriousness of the Bible, much of the church is choosing . . . to become more light and shallow and entertainment oriented, and therefore successful in its irrelevance to massive suffering and evil. The popular God of fun-church is simply too small and affable to hold a hurricane in His hand. The biblical categories of God's sovereignty lie like land mines in the pages of the Bible waiting for someone to seriously open the book. They don't kill, but they do explode trivial notions of the Almighty.[12]

If you're still entertaining such notions about the God of the Bible, you might as well stop reading right now—You'll likely not make it to the end of the book.

### It's Our Fault

So, why tsunamis? Why earthquakes, hurricanes, tornadoes, floods, volcanic eruptions and the like? Why this disruption and chaos in the world? What is the origin of all this disorder? Is the Designer at fault? Do we have a defective creation? If we read the Bible with only average comprehension skills, we know how to answer God's accusers. God tells us through the pen of the Apostle in Romans 8:19-22 . . .

> For the anxious longing of the creation waits eagerly for the revealing of the sons of God. For the creation was subjected to futility, not willingly, but because of Him who

> subjected it, in hope that the creation itself also will be set free from its slavery to corruption into the freedom of the glory of the children of God. For we know that the whole creation groans and suffers the pains of childbirth together until now.

There is much we could say here but in the interest of brevity, simply—What is the inescapable take-away? The created order has been "subjected to futility and corruption" and "groans and suffers the pains of childbirth. . . ." Who did this subjecting? God. Why? Because of man's rebellion against Him. The world is not messed up because God and His design are messed up; the world is messed up because we messed up. God put us in paradise. We wanted *more*. We got it—decay, disease, pain, death, natural disaster, etc., etc.

## Narcissistic Audacity

And yes, of course, this is the narcissistic audacity of mankind that we now enthusiastically blame God for all the *more,* even though we brought it down on ourselves—all the disorder and upheaval in this broken, fallen, judged, condemned world. Yes, much (if not most) of humanity impugns God for the consequences of our own conscious disobedience. I mean really, can you believe the self-consumed insolence of our species? Yes, the mind boggles as the caught-red-handed-guilty insurgents assert their victimhood!

After the insurrection, God said, "cursed is the ground because of you."[13] Did you hear it? The ground is cursed because of us. Because of you and me. Check the mirror, friend. Have a little intellectual integrity. Every form of calamity in this fallen world lands at your feet and mine. You know, stand up and own it. Take responsibility. The tectonic plates have been "cursed, subjected to futility, enslaved to corruption, and groan" under the weight of 7.6 billion rebels! That's on you and me. Please, stop blaming God! I'm doing you a huge favor here. It will not go well for those who accuse their Maker. Thinking people don't engage in such wrath-incurring behavior. If you have even the vaguest notion of a Supreme Being, you know your wisest course is to, yeah, shut up—sooner, rather than later. Peruse chapters 40 to 46 of Isaiah and wisely choose to put your hand over your mouth. As Francis Chan writes, ". . . when you get your own universe, you can make your own standards . . . let's not assume it's His reasoning that needs correction."[14] Amen!

## God is Dreadfully Provoked

Just as most modern pulpits eschew the high sovereignty of God, they also abstain from proclaiming the holy and fierce wrath of His righteous judgment. This biblical truth is mostly unknown to the secular world and mostly ignored by pseudo-Christian denominations. The Scriptures say . . .

> Wail, for the day of the LORD is near! It will come as destruction from the Almighty. Therefore all hands will fall limp and every man's heart will melt. They will be terrified. . . . Behold, the day of the LORD is coming, cruel, with fury and burning anger. . . . The heavens will tremble, and the earth will be shaken from its place at the fury of the LORD of hosts in the day of His burning anger.[15]

Yeah, if you haven't shut up yet, that text might give you pause.

God's not just a little miffed at the rebellion of mankind. As eighteenth-century American theologian Jonathan Edwards said in his famous sermon *Sinners in the Hands of an Angry God,* "God is dreadfully provoked."[16] These are the other attributes of God to note in this discussion—His holiness and His wrath. He will keep His promise to judge His enemies. God is sovereign; He holds the tsunami in His hand. God is holy. The tsunami is the natural outworking of His wrath against mankind's sin. Hold on to these attributes of God as we continue to biblically address

His glory in calamity, namely, His sovereignty, holiness, and wrath. You'll need them.

## Unspeakably Heinous, Monstrous, and Horrific

I do so love to watch Christian apologists on YouTube taking on the critics and skeptics. But when the *why* questions come regarding disaster and upheaval in the world, I don't recall ever hearing this, that the world is under the judgment of a provoked God because of our sin against Him. I don't think I've ever heard that put forth. I must confess, I am always dumbfounded. This is not an obscure truth in the Word of God. Sin against an infinitely good, holy, righteous, benevolent, and just God is unspeakably heinous, monstrous, and horrific. So much so, that God's judicial response not only fell upon man, but upon all creation—as is clearly revealed in the eighth chapter of Romans. God means for mankind to understand that natural disasters, along with all other forms of disorder in the universe, are not some flaw in the created order. They are evidence of our guilt before God. They are His righteous judgements against us. Regarding suffering, whether it be personal or communal, again, Piper nails it . . .

> . . . the sufferings of this life are part of a universal, God-decreed collapse of creation into disorder because of sin. God has subjected the world to futility because of sin. . . . Therefore all the misery in the world—and it is great—is a bloody declaration about the ghastly horror of sin. . . . All natural evil is a statement about the horror of moral evil. . . . Calamities are God's previews of what sin deserves and will one day receive in judgment [but] a thousand times worse. They are warnings . . . God mercifully shouts to us in . . . calamities: Wake up! Sin is like this! Sin leads to things like this. . . . The natural world is shot through with horrors to wake us from the dream-world of thinking sin is no big deal. It is a horrifically big deal.[17]

All the disorder in our world is a physical picture of the moral disorder. Natural disasters are a foreshadowing of the supernatural, eternal calamity awaiting every impenitent soul. Fifty-five million people die every year. Each death is a clarion call to the hard truth that the "wages of sin is death."[18] We've all earned our wages. Death is coming for all of us. Whether we die in our beds at 100 years of age or we're swept away by a 100-foot wall of water—that's God's business. You can critique Him if you like, but He gives life and He takes it. He does not apologize to His creatures for executing His perfect justice when, where, and how He sees fit. Yes, it's another opportune time to keep that hand over that mouth.

So, is the Bible saying the Indian Ocean tsunami was the result of sin? Yes, unequivocally. Did the sin of the Indonesians, Indians, Sri Lankans and others warrant such a catastrophe? Yes, without question—but understand, no more than your sin or my sin deserves such a disaster. Their sin was no greater than ours. Every day we wake up, we deserve calamity, disaster, and death. We are never sure when or how God will present our wages to us but we all deserved a tsunami yesterday. God says, "My wrath is being revealed from heaven against all ungodliness and unrighteousness of men. . . ."[19] Calamity and death are the outworking of His wrath owing to our rebellion against Him. Natural disaster is not a mystery. It is the prefiguring of eternal calamity. God's judgment in the natural realm is warning us about the reality and severity of His judgment in the supernatural realm—hell . . . the ultimate, eternal, and infinite calamity.

## Misplaced Amazement

It's true, mankind is guilty of a peculiar kind of misplaced amazement. If we read and comprehend our Bibles, we understand that we should not be astonished the day calamity comes; we should be astonished every day that it does not come! Every day tragedy does not befall us is the sheer mercy, forbearance, kindness, and longsuffering of God. As I once heard American theologian R. C. Sproul say, "We are shocked at justice and presume upon grace." We presume we deserve a pleasant afternoon, when God has clearly told us what our sin has earned us—death. If we have a pleasant afternoon, God has been infinitely gracious. If death comes for us, it's wages earned. As has often been said, "Who praises God for a day of wrath withheld?" Misplaced amazement indeed! Every one of us deserves to be in hell the day before yesterday!

In Romans 2:4-6, Paul writes,

> . . . Do you think lightly of the riches of His kindness and tolerance and patience, not knowing that the kindness of God leads you to repentance? But because of your stubbornness and unrepentant heart you are storing up wrath for yourself in the day of wrath and revelation of the righteous judgment of God, who will render to each person according to his deeds. . . .

We understand. Romans 1:18 is right. It's happening. God's wrath is being ". . . revealed from heaven against all ungodliness and unrighteousness of men. . . ." Today, worldwide, 152,000 individuals will die. Death is the outworking of wrath. Also, we understand. Romans 2:4 is right. It's happening. God's forbearance and mercy are everywhere evident leading many to repentance. It is clear that both Romans 2:4 forbearance, and Romans 1:18 wrath are happening every day. God is saving, and God is judging. Every natural disaster bears the marks of both God's wrath and His grace. Romans 8:19-22 clearly alludes to this reality.

> . . . the creation waits eagerly for the revealing of the sons of God . . . [being] set free from its slavery to corruption into the freedom of the glory of the children of God. For . . . the whole creation groans and suffers the pains of childbirth together until now.

In and through His righteous judgment of sin, God is working re-creation. In the midst of wrath, God is working rebirth and resurrection. Yes, natural calamity is part of the deep throes of a planet subjected to futility. But God is also working for His glory in the coming glory of His sons. God is wonderfully and mysteriously adept at bringing glory out of catastrophe. Just look at the Cross. Indeed, everything does say "Glory!"

## Living on Borrowed Time

One day Jesus is preaching about man's guilt and accountability before God, warning His hearers that they will ultimately be judged and should make peace with God while they have the opportunity. Then the question comes from the crowd about several local events that had taken multiple lives. Jesus replies:

> . . . Do you suppose that these Galileans were greater sinners than all other Galileans because they suffered this fate? I tell you, no, but unless you repent, you will all likewise perish. Or do you suppose that those eighteen on whom the tower of Siloam fell and killed them were worse culprits than all the men who live in Jerusalem? I tell you, no, but unless you repent, you will all likewise perish.[20]

Jesus doesn't speak to the theological foundation of calamity and death, that being God's judgment against mankind's rebellion. He simply underscores God's gracious message to the living in the face of such calamity and death—repent! He says those who died in the disasters were no more guilty than those who survived them or observed them. Piper again: "No, the sin of those upon whom the tower fell was not extraordinarily horrible. . . . It was ordinarily horrible. . . . Just like yours!"[21] Every day your sin and mine is horrific before a pristinely holy God. It's ordinarily heinous! It's ordinarily monstrous!

Jesus is saying to you and me that we deserve for a tower to fall on us, or for a tsunami to swallow us up, or cancer to consume us, etc. The wages of sin are never not death. Jesus is trying to relieve us of the burden of misplaced amazement. We shouldn't be amazed that people die whether by natural causes, man-made or natural disaster. We should be amazed God has graciously given us another day. The truly astonishing thing on this fallen planet today is not that we die, but that we are still walking around. It's Romans 2:4. This is divine mercy. Jesus is lovingly reminding all of us that we are living on borrowed time.

## Wake Up!

In short, when calamity, disaster, upheaval, cataclysm, and death come, it is God's thunderclap of warning to every witness—wake up from your spiritual stupor and be reconciled to your Creator! Men arrogantly and mistakenly believe that a long, healthy life is their due. They are wrong. Wrath is their due. Another day of life is always undisguised mercy. God owes us nothing but our wages. He doesn't preserve the lives of sinful men for one more day because He ought to. He does it because He is a longsuffering God. Calamity of any kind is always a wake-up call for us to deal with ultimate reality—to shock us out of our Satan-inspired, me-centered illusions about this life—to wake us up to the horrific nature of our sin before a holy God and to cause the thinking person to run to the Cross of Jesus Christ. God says, "As I live! I take no pleasure in the death of the wicked, but rather that the wicked turn from his way and live. Turn back, turn back from your evil ways! Why then will you die. . . ?"[22]

Parenthetically, how do we speak about born-again Christians that perish in natural calamity? Well, biblically I hope. We acknowledge that God is sovereign in both life and death, He "kills and makes alive."[23] We know that in this fallen world we are not exempt from "tribulations."[24] We understand that God "ordains our days when as yet there was not one of them."[25] We trust that He "causes all things to work together for good to those who love God."[26] We love that "precious in the sight of LORD is the death of His godly ones."[27] And yes, of course, we believe that "to live is Christ and to die is gain!"[28] There is an ocean of theology here. Suffice to say, we trust our Creator-Redeemer God with our lives and our deaths. Close parentheses.

## God's Awful Majesty and Dreadful Greatness

Therefore, natural disaster is not an indictment upon God but upon man. God is guilty of no wrong. We are. The point of every calamity is to remind us of the horror of our sin, the reality of God's righteous wrath, the inevitability of our own death, and God's merciful call to the living, ". . . unless you repent, you will all likewise perish."[29] How does the tsunami say "Glory!"? God is glorified in meting out His perfect justice as He meticulously renders to "each person according to his deeds."[30] And God is glorified in His breathtaking and unfathomable grace in "bringing many sons to glory."[31]

Yes, of course, all that has been said here is foolishness to the natural man.[32] It is, as Piper preaches, ". . . ludicrous to those who put the life of man above the glory of God."[33] That is not a mistake the Bible makes. Jonathan Edwards writes . . .

> It is a proper and excellent thing for infinite glory to shine forth; and for the same reason, it is proper that the shining forth of God's glory should be complete; that is, that all parts of his glory should shine forth, that every beauty should be proportionably effulgent [radiant], that the beholder may have a proper notion of God. Thus, it is necessary, that God's awful majesty, his authority and dreadful greatness, justice, and holiness, should be manifested.[34]

Yes, even in the face of calamity, that famed musician and lover of God got it right, "Everything says, 'Glory!'"

* * *

"What if God, although willing to demonstrate His wrath and to make His power known, endured with much patience vessels of wrath prepared for destruction? And He did so to make known the riches of His glory upon vessels of mercy, which He prepared beforehand for glory. . . ."[35]

*Paul, God's Apostle*

# Notes: Epilogue

[1] Isaiah 45:5-7, 9.
[2] Isaiah 55:8-9.
[3] 1 Chronicles 29:11, Psalm 103:19.
[4] Daniel 4:35.
[5] Isaiah 14:27.
[6] Ephesians 1:11, 1 Timothy 6:15-16.
[7] Revelation 19:6.
[8] Matthew 10:29.
[9] Proverbs 16:33.
[10] Mark 4:41.
[11] Amos 3:6.
[12] John Piper, *Suffering and the Sovereignty of God* (Wheaton, IL: Crossway Books, 2006),18.
[13] Genesis 3:17.
[14] Francis Chan, *Crazy Love* (Colorado Springs, CO: David C. Cook Publishing, 2008), 34.
[15] Isaiah 13:6-13, (Excerpts).
[16] Jonathan Edwards, *Sinners in the Hands of an Angry God* (New Kensington PA: Whitaker House 1997), 31.
[17] John Piper, Sermon, Bethlehem Baptist Church, Minneapolis, MN.
[18] Romans 6:23.
[19] Romans 1:18.
[20] Luke 13:2-5.
[21] John Piper, Sermon, Bethlehem Baptist Church, Minneapolis, MN.
[22] Ezekiel 33:11.
[23] 1 Samuel 2:6, Job 1:21.
[24] John 16:33.
[25] Psalm 139:16.
[26] Romans 8:28.
[27] Psalm 116:15.
[28] Philippians 1:21.
[29] Luke 13:3,5.
[30] Romans 2:6.
[31] Hebrews 2:10.
[32] I Corinthians 2:14.
[33] John Piper, Sermon, Bethlehem Baptist Church, Minneapolis, MN.
[34] Serno Dwight, *The Works of President Edwards*, Volume 8. (Leeds, England: G & C & H Carvill, 1811), 392.
[35] Romans 9:22-23.

# ~appendix~

## A Word to the Skeptic & Nominal Christian

"In the beginning was the Word, and the Word was with God, and the Word was God. He was in the beginning with God. All things came into being through Him, and apart from Him nothing came into being that has come into being. In Him was life, and the life was the Light of men. The Light shines in the darkness, and the darkness did not comprehend it."

"And the Word became flesh, and dwelt among us, and we saw His glory, glory as of the only begotten from the Father, full of grace and truth."[1]

*John, God's Apostle*

I wrote this book to Christians. Real Christians. The authentic "born of the Spirit"[2] Christians who know, and love, and walk with Jesus Christ. I've written to disciples, not to skeptics, nor to nominal church members.

It is likely, however, that this book will end up in the hands of a fair number of unbelievers and those who are merely religious. The following words are for your consideration.

While I believe there is sufficient truth and light within these pages to cause the thoughtful person to see his or her urgent need to be reconciled to their Creator, please allow me to be a bit more direct for any who might be interested in knowing more.

As noted in Chapter 7, it's not that men don't know; it's that they *do* know. God could not be more clear in the first chapter of the letter called Romans in the New Testament. You know God is there, but you're just not inclined to seek Him, submit to Him, and worship Him. This is not really about anything other than your own hard-hearted obstinance. Your Creator has said it, and ultimately, you know that it is true. You are suppressing . . .

> . . . the truth in unrighteousness, because that which is known about God is evident within [you]; God made it evident to [you]. . . . For since the creation of the world His invisible attributes, His eternal power and divine nature have been clearly seen, being understood through what has been made, so that [you] are without excuse. For even though they knew God, they did not honor Him as God, or give thanks. . . .[3]

Can't run and hide from that. You know your Creator-God is there, but you have not honored Him nor given thanks to Him.

With your continued antipathy or mere indifference toward God you are, quite literally, "storing up wrath for yourself in the day of wrath and revelation of the righteous judgment of God, who will render to every man according to His deeds."[4]

So, you have a very obvious and very simple decision to make. Will you bow your knee to this awesome galaxy-breathing Creator-God we've been talking about in this book or not? It's your call. Do you want to live now, and forever? Or, do you prefer to remain dead now, and forever? The biblical gospel is a stunning proposition. God invites any, and all, into life through His atoning work upon the cross. Again, it's entirely up to you.

Through His prophets God has said, "I permitted Myself to be sought by those who did not ask for Me; I permitted Myself to be found by those who did not seek Me. I said, Here am I, here am I. . . . I take no pleasure in the death of the wicked but rather that the wicked turn from his way and live. Turn back, turn back from your evil ways! Why then will you die…?"[5]

And Jesus said, "For God so loved the world, that He gave His only begotten Son, that whoever believes in Him should not perish but have eternal life."[6] So you see, the ball in clearly in your court. You have an open invitation to be reconciled to your Creator against whom you have rebelled.

So how is this reconciliation effected? "By grace, through faith"[7] in the Person and work of Jesus Christ. I'm sure you know the story, if not, read the Gospel of John. It's only 21 chapters—the most important 21 chapters you will have ever read! John wrote his Gospel in order that "you may believe that Jesus is the Christ, the Son of God; and that believing you may have life in His name."[8]

And of course, biblical conversion is not merely believing historical facts about Jesus Christ. Satan and every last demon believe the facts. True Christianity is believing in such a way that everything changes from the inside out. Jesus Christ said it: "Unless one is born again, he cannot see the kingdom of God."[9]And His Apostle described it like this: ". . . if any man is in Christ, he is a new creature; the old things have passed away; behold, new things have come."[10]

Biblical Christianity is always a supernatural miracle of God evidenced by a radical and conspicuous change in the life. No one who is born again stays the same. If it's real, it all changes. The new life of God within will spill out into your everyday life. It's not hard to know if you're born again; in fact, it's impossible not to know. If you're a genuine Christian you will love Jesus Christ supremely. You will understand, love, embrace, and seek to incarnate the Apostle's words: "to live is Christ and to die is gain."[11] Yes, He is that beautiful; He is that compelling!

So, what's the proper religious formula to get yourself sorted out with God? How do you go from lost to found? How does one who is headed to an eternal hell change that eternity? Obey God! Do what He says! Repent of your sin, self-love, and rebellion against Him, and place your faith in Jesus Christ as your Lord and Savior. You believe He is God. You believe that His death on the cross atoned for your sin. You believe you are saved by grace through faith in Jesus Christ and His saving work.

You say, "Jim, I don't know anything about the the Word of God or His offer of salvation through Jesus Christ." Well then, get yourself a Bible, find a real Christian, and a real Bible-believing, Bible-preaching church, and begin the journey. Because "faith comes by hearing, and hearing by the word of Christ."[12] And here is the breathtaking promise of your Creator-God: ". . . you will seek Me and find Me, when you search for Me with all your heart. And I will be found by you declares the LORD. . . ."[13]

And God says, "[I]f you confess with your mouth Jesus as Lord and believe in your heart that God raised Him from the dead, you shall be saved; for with the heart man believes resulting in righteousness and with the mouth he confesses resulting in salvation."[14]Yeah, God's offer is there. His conditions are there. It's your call!

* * *

"And this is eternal life, that they may know You, the only true God, and Jesus Christ whom You have sent."[15]
*Jesus Christ, God Incarnate*

# Notes: Appendix

[1] John 1:1-5, 14
[2] John 3:5-8
[3] Romans 1:18-21
[4] Romans 2:5-6
[5] Isaiah 65:1, Ezekiel 33:11
[6] John 3:16
[7] Ephesians 2:8
[8] John 20:31
[9] John 3:3
[10] 2 Corinthian 5:17
[11] Philippians 1:21
[12] Romans 10:17
[13] Jeremiah 29:13-14
[14] Romans 10:9-10
[15] John 17:3

# About the Author

At the age of 42, Jim left a twenty-year business career to answer God's call to preach. Since early 2004, he and his wife, Karen, have lived in Milan, Italy, where Jim is the pastor of the International Church of Milan, a non-denominational, Bible-believing, and Bible-teaching church ministering to internationals from every corner of the globe. He is also author of *Uncareful Lives: Walking Where Feet May Fail.*

Also by Jim Albright

*Uncareful Lives: Walking Where Feet May Fail*

ISBN 9781620205303

Warning: reading this book can be hazardous to your health. And your wealth. And your plans. And more. As Alex and Brett Harris urged teenaged Christians to do hard things, so Jim Albright exhorts all believers in Christ to live uncareful lives. He does this by walking through the lives of the heroic believers portrayed in Hebrews 11, noting that their names are not indelibly etched into this chapter because they always followed the common admonition to be careful, but because they did just the opposite. They were not reckless, rather they were simply willing to take God at His Word. Read this book, and you may find that, like those exemplars of faith, you begin to live a more uncareful life for the glory of God too.
*Donald S. Whitney, Professor of Biblical Spirituality, The Southern Baptist Theological Seminary*

Learn more about *Uncareful Lives* at
http://www.uncarefullives.com/

You can find Jim's sermons at
https://pastorjimpodcast.podbean.com/

CPSIA information can be obtained
at www.ICGtesting.com
Printed in the USA
BVHW040752120219
539956BV00024BA/3282/P